A Valiant Ign

Vol. 3

Mary Angela Dickens

Alpha Editions

This edition published in 2024

ISBN : 9789362094520

Design and Setting By
Alpha Editions
www.alphaedis.com
Email - info@alphaedis.com

As per information held with us this book is in Public Domain.
This book is a reproduction of an important historical work. Alpha Editions uses the best technology to reproduce historical work in the same manner it was first published to preserve its original nature. Any marks or number seen are left intentionally to preserve its true form.

Contents

CHAPTER I .... - 1 -
CHAPTER II .... - 6 -
CHAPTER III .... - 18 -
CHAPTER IV .... - 28 -
CHAPTER V .... - 37 -
CHAPTER VI .... - 46 -
CHAPTER VII .... - 50 -
CHAPTER VIII .... - 54 -
CHAPTER IX .... - 61 -
CHAPTER X .... - 69 -
CHAPTER XI .... - 74 -
CHAPTER XII .... - 79 -
CHAPTER XIII .... - 86 -
CHAPTER XIV .... - 98 -
CHAPTER XV .... - 105 -
CHAPTER XVI .... - 112 -

CHAPTER I

It was not generally known among his acquaintances that Marston Loring had come back from Africa accompanied by a new friend; this new friend was not introduced by Loring at either of his clubs, and yet the two met at least once every day. He was a man named Alfred Ramsay; a small, insignificant-looking man, with sandy hair, which had turned—in streaks—the peculiar grey which such hair assumes, and small, dull eyes that never seemed to move in his head.

It was nearly three o'clock on the afternoon following that on which Loring had called on Mrs. Romayne, and he and his new friend were together in his chambers in the Temple. Mr. Ramsay had been there several times before, and he was sitting now in an arm-chair in the sunshine with an air of total want of interest in his surroundings, which was characteristic of him. Loring was walking up and down the room thoughtfully.

"Romayne!" observed Ramsay. "Not a particularly good name on the market! It belonged to a first-class swindler twenty years ago—William Romayne. This young gentleman is no connexion, I suppose?"

The remark broke a short silence, and Loring stopped in his walk and leant back against the mantelpiece as he answered.

"Yes," he said tersely, "he's his son. He has never been in his father's line, though—I doubt whether he knows anything about him, though it's an odd thing that he shouldn't! As to the name, why, it's an old story, and won't affect any one nowadays, I take it. The point is that he has this respectable capital, and is—exceedingly keen on increasing it."

There was a dryness in Loring's voice as he said the last words, which implied a great deal more than did his words. And it was apparently to that significance that the other man replied.

"A chip of the old block," said Ramsay musingly. "I wonder, now, how far it goes?"

The last words were spoken very slowly, and the dull eyes looked straight before them.

Loring looked down at him with a cynical smile just touching his lips. He knew considerably more about his new friend's character than he would have chosen to put into words, and he could guess, not inaccurately, what was passing in his mind at the moment. And the realisation of the shadowy possibilities with which Ramsay was occupied was no part of Marston Loring's designs. He made no direct answer.

"He should be here by this time," he said carelessly.

And as he spoke there was a sharp, cheery rap at the door; it opened quickly, and Julian Romayne appeared, very boyish, very good-looking, and with a curious, veiled keenness in his eyes.

"We were just expecting you," said Loring, greeting him with a friendly nod. "Let me introduce you to Mr. Alfred Ramsay."

Mr. Alfred Ramsay had risen to honour the introduction, turning his whole head slowly round as he looked at Julian, so that his eyes still gazed straight before them as they rested on the young man's face.

"Pleased to know you," he said indifferently.

"Very glad to make your acquaintance," responded Julian pleasantly. "I hope I'm not behind time?"

"Pretty fair," said Loring, laying his hand on the young man's shoulder with kindly patronage. "But Ramsay is a busy man, you know, so suppose we get to business at once. Ramsay," he continued, in a brisk, businesslike voice, as the three sat down about the table, "Romayne knows nothing of the affair whatever. I shall begin by running over the preliminaries with him. And, first of all," he went on, turning to Julian, "of course it is understood, Romayne, that we keep the matter to ourselves."

He spoke in a curt, off-hand manner, and as Julian made a quick gesture of acquiescence, he went on in the same businesslike tone.

"I don't know whether you know anything about the Welcome Diamond Mining Company?" he said. "Probably not. It was floated about this time last year, and the greater part of the business came into my hands. The shares were taken up all right, but—well, it didn't come to anything, and its affairs had something to do with my going out to the Cape. It was in connection with those same affairs that I and Ramsay met."

Julian had listened so far with a clouded countenance, and now, as Loring paused, he leant back in his chair with a movement of irrepressible disappointment.

"Oh!" he said shortly. "It's a mine, then?"

"There is a mine in connection with it," replied Loring imperturbably. "But you need not trouble yourself about the mine. That is only the figure-head, you understand. The affair itself is a matter of—arrangement. Look here, Romayne," he went on, as Julian leant suddenly forward across the table, "shares in the Welcome Diamond Mining Company are at this moment worth about five shillings each."

He paused. He had been leaning carelessly back in his chair, and now he moved, uncrossing his legs, and leaning one arm on the table.

"In a few days," he went on deliberately and significantly, "they will fall to two shillings." He paused again, with a slight, matter-of-course gesture. "That will be worked, of course," he said.

Julian nodded comprehension.

"Yes?" he said.

"At that price," continued Loring, "all the shares will be bought up by two or three men, in consequence of private information received from the Cape."

The last words came from Loring slowly and deliberately, and his eyes met Julian's significantly. A quick flash of understanding passed across Julian's face, and Loring continued easily:

"Reports to this effect will get about. The fact of the presence in London of a mining engineer from the vicinity of the Welcome will also get about. Perhaps he may allow himself to be interviewed, you know—nothing definite, of course. The shares will go up with a run."

He paused, and Julian threw himself back in his chair, tapping the table meditatively with one hand. His gaze was fixed upon the wall just over Loring's head, and there was a curious expression on his face which combined the keen matter-of-fact calculation of the habitual speculator with a certain unconscious gleam of hungry excitement which was eloquent of youth and inexperience. A minute or two passed, during which Mr. Ramsay's eyes rested indifferently on the young man's face, and then Julian spoke. His voice, also, in spite of his evident attempt at emulation of Loring's businesslike nonchalance, was just touched by that youthful incapacity for holding keen personal interest in abeyance.

"And the private information received from the Cape will be supplied——?" he said interrogatively.

"Will be supplied by Ramsay," returned Loring.

The words were spoken with the slightest possible movement of the eyelids. Julian made a quick gesture of comprehension, and there was a moment's silence. Then Loring went on crisply, darting a quick glance at Julian's face in its calculating eagerness.

"In a private speculation of this kind, of course, it is a case of working together and share and share alike. Now, we propose—Ramsay and I, you understand—to make up a joint capital for the purchase of these shares. We are prepared to put into it fifteen thousand pounds between us, and we want another ten thousand at least. If you are prepared to put in that sum, or more, on the understanding that the profits—after each man has received back his original investment—are divided into three equal shares, we are willing to take you in with us."

Julian looked up at him quickly.

"Into three equal shares?" he said, with a stress on the adjective.

"Into three equal shares," returned Loring drily. "Capital is not the sole requisite in this affair, and the other factors are supplied by Ramsay and myself."

A dark flush mounted to Julian's forehead, and the avidity in his eyes developed.

"It's a large order, though," he said. "I don't quite see where I come in at that rate, after all."

Loring leant back in his chair and looked him full in the face.

"You can please yourself, of course," he said. "Take it or leave it. You will come in to the tune of something like thirty thousand. If you see your way to trebling your capital by any other means, do so. Lots of fellows will be glad to take your place with us."

Julian's eyes gleamed greedily, and he wavered obviously.

"Those are your final terms?" he said.

"Our final terms," said Loring concisely, looking at Ramsay, who nodded nonchalantly in confirmation of the words.

A silence ensued. Julian sat staring down at the table, his brows knit, evidently in close thought. At last he glanced up suddenly at the two men who had been waiting carelessly for his decision.

"I call it rather rough," he said brusquely; "but—all right. If the thing looks all right when you've trotted it out, I accept."

He passed on instantly, with a brief, telling question, to the inner working of the scheme.

There is perhaps nothing by which self-revelation is more frankly and unconsciously made than through the means by which a man may be most easily roused to enthusiasm. Enthusiasm—a genuine quickening of his mental pulses, even—had been a condition of things practically unknown to the easy-going, commonplace Julian Romayne of a year before; but in the course of the last two months he had experienced it often. To hear of large sums of money, large profits, rapid returns on striking investments, touched him, instinctively, as a record of artistic achievements will touch an artist, as triumphs of research will touch an historian, as prodigies of physical prowess will touch an athlete. And as Loring answered him now, and went on with fuller and more technical detail, his face changed strikingly. His eyes brightened, and an eager, fascinated light came into them; he leant farther forward, listening, commenting, questioning, with quick and always increasing excitement.

Half an hour passed, and still the three men sat about the table, talking in terse, businesslike fashion; three-quarters of an hour, an hour. At the end of that time, Julian, his face flushed and eager, his eyes glistening and sparkling, his hand absolutely shaking with excitement, was holding that hand out to Mr. Ramsay with a gesture which witnessed to the work of that hour, as volumes could not have done. As far as words went, he and Mr. Ramsay had hardly exchanged three sentences; it was the bond that lay behind the words that had drawn them together. Mr. Ramsay had spoken very little, indeed, but his silent presence had never for a moment seemed superfluous, or without a certain indefinite weight; and there was a dull approval in his slow eyes now as he turned them on the young man.

"We've settled so much, then," said Julian, in a quick, familiar way, "and we meet here on Thursday at two. Until then———" He turned to Loring, and stretched out his hand eagerly. "Thanks, old man," he said in a low, quick voice. "Thanks."

CHAPTER II

MISS Pomeroy's visit to Mrs. Romayne was postponed for a fortnight. At one time, indeed, it seemed not impossible that Mrs. Pomeroy's visit to her sister in Devonshire might be postponed indefinitely, and Mrs. Romayne was charmingly inconsolable over her prospective disappointment.

It was a delightful thing to have a girl in the house! Mrs. Romayne made the discovery and the statement as the very first evening of Miss Pomeroy's stay with her drew to a close. And certainly, the evening, signalised by a little dinner-party, had been pleasant enough to warrant satisfaction. Julian had been in the best possible spirits, elated apparently by the presence of his mother's visitor, at whose side he was to be found whenever his duties as host allowed such concentration of his attention. Miss Pomeroy herself had been a model of gentle amiability, and had looked more than usually bright and pretty. Loring, who had made one of the dinner guests, had also been at his best and most amusing. No conversation of any length had, of course, been possible between him and his hostess; but a quick, low-toned word or two passed between them in the movement that ensued upon the reappearance of the men in the drawing-room after dinner.

And on the tone of that first evening, that of the fortnight into which Miss Pomeroy's stay lengthened itself was modelled. They were very dissipated, Mrs. Romayne asserted laughingly; and she further declared that she had never enjoyed dissipation so much. Julian's hard-working impulses seemed to be in partial abeyance for the time being; their demands on him, though peremptory when they did occur, did not prevent a great deal of attendance on his mother and her guest. Loring also seemed hardly to have settled back into his usual routine, and frequently made one of the party. His appearance on the scene, and the recognition of that compact between them which he never failed to make, either by a glance or a few quiet words, were never without a certain effect on Mrs. Romayne; not on her spirits, for they never varied in their gaiety; but on a hard restlessness in her eyes, always lessened for the moment by that look or word from Loring.

The last day of June was also the last day of Mrs. Pomeroy's absence from London, and it was, moreover, the day fixed for a certain dance which was to stand out from all the other dances of the season. The givers of this dance were parvenus of the most pronounced type, and during the past three seasons, they had paid their way into London society by spending fortunes on the entertainments they gave. This season they had issued cards of invitation, on which each guest was requested to wear mediæval Florentine dress, and it had been whispered abroad that thousands were to be spent in providing such a setting for these costumes as should eclipse anything hitherto seen. Fortunately for the projectors—and nobody knew better than they how absolutely impossible it was to calculate in such a matter—the idea caught society's fancy; it was taken up with the wild enthusiasm which alternates in the modern mind with blank indifference; and as every one with an invitation had spent some three weeks in ardent consideration of his or her dress for the occasion, that occasion had acquired a fictitious importance of a colossal nature, and was absolutely looked forward to as promising something quite unusual—and equally indefinite—in the way of amusement.

The whole thing had evidently been arranged, Mrs. Romayne declared gaily, to give a final touch of triumph to the end of Maud Pomeroy's visit to her. It was about four o'clock in the afternoon of the day in question, and she and Miss Pomeroy, with Julian as escort, were taking what she described as "a little turn" in the Park when she expressed this opinion. It was a perfect June afternoon, the Park was very full, and all three seemed to be exhilarated either by the sunshine, the movement, or the prospect of the evening. The fortnight's intimate association with her present companions had apparently had no effect whatever upon Miss Pomeroy's demure conventionality of manner, but her word was readier than usual, and her expression was brighter; Mrs. Romayne talked and laughed and kept the ball of chatter going; and about Julian's hilarity there was a touch of excitement which was a characteristic which had grown upon him markedly in the course of the last month. He turned upon his mother, protesting gaily.

"That's much too depressing a point of view," he said. "It forces on us exactly what we want to forget—that it is the end. Now, I've made up my mind to cut the connection between to-night and both yesterday and to-morrow, and enjoy myself tremendously."

"And is 'cutting the connection'—it sounds as if something might blow up—an indispensable preliminary?" laughed Mrs. Romayne.

"Why, of course." He glanced at Miss Pomeroy as he spoke, and the colour deepened in her cheeks by just a shade as she turned to Mrs. Romayne and said, with one of her little smiles and a rather poor attempt at mock confidence:

"Mr. Romayne wants to forget the terrific anxiety which he has already suffered over that gorgeous dress of his, and the terrific bill from which he has still to suffer."

Julian's protestations were as eager and boyish in manner as they were delicate and skilful in matter, and Mrs. Romayne broke in upon them with a laughing apology and a request that Julian would tell the coachman to turn out into Piccadilly and drive to a house in Grosvenor Place. Julian gave the order, and added to it:

"You can pull up when you get out of the Park."

Mrs. Romayne took up the words instantly.

"Are you not coming with us, bad boy?" she said. "Come and help us pay one call, at any rate. We are going straight home after that to prepare ourselves for the triumphs of the evening by a little refreshing laziness, are we not, Maud?"

"I should like to immensely!" returned Julian ardently as Miss Pomeroy smiled a response. "But I'm afraid I must go down to the club. I promised to meet Loring there! Dinner at eight, I suppose?" he added as the carriage drew up and he jumped out.

He stepped back on the pavement, lifting his hat as the carriage drove off. Then he jumped into a hansom and gave the word to drive, not to the club but to the Temple. Arrived there he ran upstairs, the excitement about him gaining ground moment by moment, to Marston Loring's rooms. Loring was there alone. He was seated at the writing-table writing rapidly, his face keen and intent, and he suspended his work for an instant only as he glanced up on the opening of the door and nodded a greeting.

Julian's life for the last month had been lived at that high pressure which is only produced in a man by the consciousness that he has burnt his ships. Every shilling that he had accumulated during the previous six months was invested in the scheme propounded to him a month ago by Marston Loring; and the history of his real life during the interval would have been a history of the stages through which that scheme had passed. The affairs of the Welcome Diamond Mining Company had followed precisely the course indicated by Loring during that first interview on the subject between Loring, Ramsay, and Julian. Shortly after that interview "Welcomes" had fallen to a nominal price; they had then been bought up according to arrangement. A slight rise had followed as a matter of course, followed by an interval of vacillation, and a slow succession of trifling advances, which had again been succeeded by a period of quiet.

So far the excitement with which every hour had been instinct for Julian had been the excitement of preparation solely; the ground had been tilled and the seed sown. And what that soil was in which he had sown his seed; what were the characteristics that were to prove so stimulating; it was not in him to consider. He was perfectly well aware of the nature of the transaction in which he was engaged; he had understood at the outset that the "private information received from the Cape" on which the shares were to be bought up was a "put up thing," as he would have expressed it, between Ramsay and Marston Loring; and the knowledge affected him not at all. That black thread in the warp of his character was running strong and deep now, and to such considerations his sensibilities were absolutely dormant.

"Well?" The monosyllable broke from him eager and impetuous, as though it contained the pent-up suspense and excitement of hours. He had come up rapidly to Loring's side, and the latter, without lifting his eyes, signed to an evening paper which lay on the table as he said briefly:

"All right!"

Julian's face turned quite white; he snatched up the paper and turned with breathless eagerness to the column devoted to the money market.

"Welcome Diamond Company Shares."

The blue eyes seemed to leap at the line and fasten on it with a hungry avidity pitiful to see, and he stood there gazing at it with glittering, fascinated eyes, with a curious stillness upon him from head to foot, as though all remembrance of his actual surroundings, all thought even of Loring, had faded. Nearly five minutes had passed when Loring laid down his pen and leant back in his chair, turning a little that he might fix his eyes on Julian as he stood rather behind him.

"Pretty fair?" he said carelessly.

Julian lifted his eyes from the paper and turned his white face to Loring. He nodded as though the feelings of the moment were not to be put into speech, and then the slow, deep colour of excitement began to creep over his features.

"Have you seen Ramsay?" he said in a low, quick voice.

"Saw him this morning. He told me things were beginning to move. It was that paragraph yesterday that did it!"

"And what about keeping it up?" said Julian. "This is the ticklish moment, I take it! What's the next move?"

He had thrown himself into a chair as he spoke; his voice was jerking with eagerness, as though some of his excitement were finding expression. Loring looked at him for an instant before he answered. He was asking himself a question which had formulated itself in his mind more than once in the last month; namely, was it merely the influence of his blood which made young Romayne so keen a speculator; or was there something concealed in the background of his life which made money a desperate necessity with him?

"This is the next move," he answered, indicating the sheets of manuscript paper which lay before him. "This will be in one or two of the papers to-morrow, and if I'm not mistaken it will have a big effect!"

Julian stretched out his hand impulsively for the sheets and ran through them, now and then breaking into an eager comment; and as he finished he rose impetuously and began to pace excitedly up and down the room. His face was flushed now, and his eyes glowing.

"Yes, that ought to take us a long way!" he said. "And Ramsay backing it up all the while, of course? Loring, what do you make of it? An affair of—weeks?"

"An affair of two or three weeks, all told!" returned Loring nonchalantly. "The inside of a month ought to put the best part of thirty thousand into each of our pockets, my boy."

He rose as he spoke, and gathered together the sheets of manuscript, but as he did so his quick ear caught a strange, sharp catch in Julian's breath. He fastened up the papers, and directed them with another of those slight smiles, and then turned again to the younger man. Julian was standing at the window staring almost stupidly out.

"I'm going to turn you out now!" said Loring lightly. "Coming down to the club with me?"

Julian turned round, but the words seemed to penetrate slowly to his consciousness.

"No!" he said at last. "No, thanks, old man. I—I'm going to get home."

He had to go to his own chambers first, it appeared, however, and Loring left him with a careless "All right! See you to-night, of course!"

The sunshine had left Julian's room, bright as it still was outside, and it looked, perhaps, the darker by contrast as he opened the door and shut himself in alone. He paused a moment, with his hand on the lock, and then walked aimlessly across to the writing-table and sat down. There was a pale, dazed look about him.

The line in the evening paper at which he had gazed with such devouring eyes had chronicled the first important rise of those shares on which his hopes were staked; chronicled, in fact, the beginning of the end. As he sat there alone, the words seemed to stand out all about him; to meet his eyes in every direction; and it was little wonder that, as he realised that the seed so eagerly sown had indeed broken ground at last, the perfect fruit seemed to be already in his hand, and he was dazed and intoxicated with anticipated triumph. He had the blood of a speculator and a gambler in his veins, and as he sprang up suddenly from his chair and began to pace up and down the room, it was the surging of the speculator's instinct that flushed his face and glittered in his eyes; the rioting of that money passion which, to the man who has never felt its fever, is the strangest and most repulsive—as it is the most abnormal—of all passions.

But little by little, without volition or even consciousness on his part, the current of his thoughts changed. Gradually that greedy, tumultuous contemplation of money as an end wavered, altered into a contemplation of money as a means, into a passing over of that means in the realisation of the end which it was to bring about. He was thinking of Clemence, thinking of her in a tumult of excitement in which the goading of that two-edged dart of love and shame which quivered always in his better nature was absolutely unfelt; thinking of her in a very hallucination of intoxicated triumph. He was living out with her a future life of triumphant satisfaction; a life so utterly incompatible with the facts of the case, with all that had come and gone, and must still come and go, as to be a most pathetic imagining; when the sound of a clock striking brought him suddenly to himself.

His first conscious thought was a certain vague surprise at his surroundings; as far as externals went he had left Loring's room and had come to his own like a man walking in his sleep. Then he realised the nature of the sound that had roused him, and drew out his watch to see what hour it was that had struck. It was seven, and the fact, with the pressing necessity for his return home which it involved, gave a turn to the current of his thoughts by which, without changing their main character, they were blended in with the actual practicalities of the moment. He thought of his mother with a certain bitter triumph. "It's not for long," he said to himself, "not for long now." His mind ran on over the details of the evening before him; the little dinner—"only ourselves," Mrs. Romayne had said gaily; the artificialities that would pass between himself and his mother; the effective flirtation which he would have to keep up with Miss Pomeroy—the flirtation which in the excitement of the past month he had carried on recklessly. And then with his hand on the door he stopped abruptly—stopped and stood quite still with a strange, defiant recklessness growing in his face. Whether it was some curious effect of the tumult through which he had passed, whether it originated in those jubilant visions of Clemence from which he had so recently awakened, it is not possible to say. But on that instant there had risen within him an impulse of fierce, overmastering repulsion against his mother, against Miss Pomeroy, against the part he had chosen to play. Almost before he had realised the sudden sense of overwhelming revolt and distaste which had seized him, its obverse was upon him. Clemence! To see Clemence! To speak to Clemence! To satisfy the hungry longing which, for the moment, seemed absolutely to possess him!

Such a longing, in various forms and degrees, had shaken and torn him often before, but hitherto something—some influence from Clemence's own words, some jarring and throbbing of that better nature in himself—had held him back. But now, strung up and carried out of himself by his excitement, he was impervious to all considerations save that of his own overmastering craving. The end was very near now, he told himself. It was a question of a week or two only. He must see her; she herself would see that it was only reasonable that he should see her!

His plans were laid in the passing of a few seconds. The only address Clemence had given him was that of the house of business where she worked—where she had worked when he met her first—his only chance of seeing her lay in meeting her when she left her work at night. He would not go home to dinner, he decided; he would telegraph to his mother, and dine at a quiet restaurant. That would bring him, as he knew well enough, to the earliest hour at which the "hands," of whom Clemence made one, were likely to be released, and he would wait in the little by-street in which the "hands'" entrance was situated until she came.

He went out of the room with a quick, assured step, sent off his telegram—a brief "Detained. Inconsolable"—from an office in Fleet Street, and then, carefully avoiding the fashionable resorts, he walked to the restaurant he had mentally selected.

The little street which, for some scores of men and women, formed the picture evoked by a name which, for the shopping population of London, involved a mental vision of a busy thoroughfare and a considerable expanse of plate-glass windows, ran parallel to that thoroughfare, divided from it only by a long block of buildings; and bearing in mind the slight nature of the division between the two, the contrast presented was almost startling. The little street was a thoroughfare inasmuch as it led from one side-street to another; but these streets were very little frequented, and the connecting-link between them was a short cut to nowhere. It represented simply so many back entrances to places of business, and these being to a great extent monopolised by a single firm, the comings and goings at stated times of the hands employed by that firm was often the only movement that broke the quiet from morning until night. In the intervals between these comings and goings there brooded over the street such a silence and stillness as seemed strangely incompatible with the thought of all the labour and effort that it held; with the hard day's work towards which those coming footsteps in the morning were bent; with the hard day's work which lay behind those departing footsteps in the evening. The street itself had a squalid, neglected look, too, as though life and activity had passed it by.

The day's work was not over yet, though the evening light was making long shadows, and the setting sun was turning the upper windows of the opposite houses into ruddy fire; the street was absolutely silent and deserted when

Julian turned quickly into it. He pulled up and surveyed his surroundings with a rapid, comprehensive glance.

It was too early yet. He looked at his watch and told himself so with somewhat over-elaborated carelessness, and took out his cigarette-case. He lighted a cigarette; and pacing slowly up and down the pavement on the opposite side of the street to that on which he expected Clemence to emerge, he began to reckon with himself the chances for and against her speedy or tardy appearance.

But such practical, matter-of-fact considerations involved a deliberate mental action on his part, and having gone through it, urged by that curious instinct under which intense excitement always desires to assert itself as absolute calm and sanity, he gradually let himself slip away again from the practical and the actual, and gave himself up to the tide of his exhilarated imaginings.

There is nothing more exciting, nothing that sooner quickens the mental pulses into a very fever of confusion, than the sudden indulgence of an impulse long resisted. The hour that had passed since the idea, of which his presence in that quiet little street was the outcome, had flashed into Julian's mind and dominated it, had carried him as completely out of himself, and out of touch with realities, as is a man under the influence of absinthe. As a man so exhilarated will be impervious to a considerable amount of physical pain, so Julian was for the time being absolutely unconscious of anything painful or shameful in his position. The circumstances under which he had parted from Clemence; all the bitter pain and longing under which he had smarted and writhed with such fierce rebellion; the attitude towards himself which his conduct might only too justly have created in his wife; were absolutely obliterated from his mind. He was waiting now—husband, master, altogether the superior; triumphant, successful, self-assured—for his mistaken but doubtless submissive wife; conscious, and rather pleased with the consciousness, that he loved her in spite of her faults.

One quarter after another chimed out from a neighbouring clock. He had been waiting nearly an hour, oblivious, in his elation, of tedium or weariness; oblivious of the claim upon him of the life of Queen Anne Street as though it had no existence for him. The slight feeling of impatience with which he realised that the fourth quarter was chiming was entirely unconnected with such externals; and it was an eloquent testimony to his mental attitude that it took the form of a faint sense of irritation with Clemence for delaying so long. A vague feeling of lordly disapproval of her conduct stirred in him, as he paused at the top of the street and glanced across at the still fast-closed doors. He was just looking dubiously at his cigarette-case when the click of a latch, instantly followed by the sound of girls' voices, made him start violently. He thrust the case hastily into his pocket and walked quickly down the street, until he was standing just opposite the door from which a little stream of girls and women was pouring forth.

Several figures had already detached themselves from the stream and were moving rapidly away, either singly or in pairs; but one quick glance told him that neither of these was Clemence, and he fixed his eyes with eager confidence on the doorway through which she had still to pass. His face was flushed with intense excitement. On came the stream, girls and women following one another in unbroken succession; pretty girls, plain girls, shabby girls, smart girls, some arm in arm, some laughing and talking in loud-voiced groups; several of these groups noticed his waiting figure and commented upon it in giggling whispers, turning back as they passed down the street to look at it again, but Julian only saw that none of these was Clemence. The stream was beginning to dwindle; stragglers followed one another now at irregular intervals; the two girls who had been the last to appear had nearly reached the end of the street, and still Julian's eyes were riveted on the open doorway.

The girls turned the corner, and down the dim passage into which he was looking there came slowly another figure quite alone. Before it had emerged into the light Julian was across the road, as though that one great throb with which his heart leapt up to meet her had impelled him physically, and as Clemence passed out into the soft dusk of the June evening he spoke her name, eagerly at first, then with a strange break in his voice:

"Clemence! Clemence!"

At the first sound of his voice—evidently the first sign to her that he was near—a low, indescribable cry broke from Clemence; she turned towards him trembling, swaying as she stood, and Julian caught her in his arms lest she should fall.

"You've come!" she cried, and before the exquisite rapture and relief of her faint, quivering voice, with all that it implied of suffering past, a harder man than Julian might have melted. "My dear, my dear, I knew you'd come! I knew! I knew!"

But that pathetic voice had not been needed. The first sight of her face as she turned it upon him with that wonderful irradiation of joy upon it, had shrivelled into nothingness all the exultation, all the triumph and self-satisfaction of the past few hours, and Julian held her in his arms, his trance over, self-convicted, self-condemned; his whole consciousness absorbed in that heavy, throbbing agony of his better nature which had leapt into sudden relentless life. What it was that so penetrated him he could not have defined. Where and in what proportion old influence revived, touched, and was blended with a heart-piercing sense of the change in her, he could not have said; he did not even know that these were indeed the powers that had struck him. The change in her, even as he gazed down at her face with agonised, remorseful eyes, as it rested for one moment on his shoulder, he rather felt than traced and understood.

That change was very great. Those past six months had dealt heavily with that thin, white face, and the marks of their passing were plain to see, even in that moment of absolute transfiguration. Every curve, every suggestion of girlishness seemed to have been worn away; worn away by those cruel twin refiners, never so pitiless as when they work together—physical suffering and mental distress. The outline of her features had lost some of its beauty in that intense accentuation; the colourless lips were slightly drawn, and under the sunken eyes were heavy shadows. But no remembrance of the physical loveliness which she had lost could stand for an instant before the spiritual loveliness which she had gained. It was as though those twin refiners, before whom nothing earthly or external can stand and flourish, had strengthened that which lay behind the externals with which they had dealt so ruthlessly. The eyes, so indescribably beautiful as they looked now into Julian's, had been beautiful even in that moment before she realised his presence; beautiful in their heaviness as no brightness, as no common happiness could have made them; beautiful with the perfect patience and dignity of accepted suffering. The tired mouth had been beautiful in its repose, as it was beautiful now in its tremulous rapture; beautiful in its quiet constancy and self-abnegation.

She let herself rest for a moment in his arms; clinging to him with something in her touch which he had never felt before; looking up into his face as her head lay back against his shoulder with a strange, tremulous, tender light quivering on every feature, shaken from head to foot by little tremulous, tearless sobs—the sobs of utter relief and peace. Then she disengaged herself gently, and drew herself away, something of that first ecstasy dying out of her face to leave it soft and happy beyond all words. That strange light still shone in her eyes, and, as she moved, one thin hand retained its clinging hold on his arm, as though some instinct of dependence influenced her involuntarily. She was dressed, not as the other girls had been, in a light summer jacket, but in a long cloak, and as she drew it about her with the other hand, the softest touch of colour came into her white cheek.

"My dear!" she said softly. "My dear!"

And Julian whispered hoarsely as he had whispered again and again:

"Clemmie! Clemmie!"

He made no attempt to take her in his arms again. Even the gesture with which he laid his hand upon those clinging fingers on his sleeve was diffident and almost tremulous; tender and reverent as no gesture of his had ever been in all his life before. He could find no words. In her presence everything—all the triumph, all that had seemed to him the necessities and realities of life—seemed to have fallen away from him. He was nothing. He had nothing! He could say nothing to her.

There was a silence; silence which for Clemence as her fingers closed round his, and that soft colour came and went in her cheeks, breathed an ineffable content; silence which for Julian held the blackest depths of self-revelation and self-contempt. It was broken at last by Clemence.

"Is it done, dear?" she said gently.

Julian's hand turned cold in hers, and his eyes fell away from her face.

"Not—not yet, Clemmie!" he faltered wretchedly. "I—I came to tell you—to tell you that——"

"That you are going to do it? That you are going to do it? My dear, my dear, you mean that? Oh, you mean that, don't you?"

She had not raised her voice or changed her pose, but that touch upon his arm had become a close, convulsive grip, and even the clutch of the worn, blanched hand upon her cloak witnessed to the agony of supplication with which every nerve was strained and quivering. Her low voice thrilled and vibrated with it; her white face, to which his first words had brought a look of heart-sick disappointment, was an embodied prayer. He could not answer on the instant; it cut him like a lash; and she went on rapidly, her low, beseeching voice breaking and trembling with the intense feeling that flickered on her face like a light.

"Julian, for my sake, for your wife's sake, dear! I love you so! I—I need you so! Don't part us any longer! If it was for your good, if it was to make you happy, there's nothing I would not face, and face cheerfully—ah, you know that, don't you? But you're doing wrong, and I think of it always, and it makes the loneliness so that I can't bear it. Oh, I can't bear it!"

She broke suddenly into low shuddering sobs and tears, and her head fell forward helplessly on to his breast, though she still kept her convulsive hold upon his arm. He put his other arm round her and drew her towards him, and as he did so he seemed to realise with a kind of double consciousness the course he would take and its utter contemptibility.

"Don't, Clemmie dear! Don't! don't!" he said in a broken, uneven voice. "It's all right, dear! I'm going to do it! I came to tell you so! It's all right!"

"You're going to—tell her?"

"I am, Clemence! I promise you I am! Only—only not for a week or two. There's—there's something I must wait for!"

"But you are going to? You are? You are?"

"On my—on my soul, yes, Clemence!"

There was a moment's silence, broken only by her low, tremulous sobs; then these too died away. At last, with a long sighing breath, she raised herself and looked into his pale, miserable face, with her own quiet and exhausted.

"Must you wait?" she said, with an indescribable accent on the first bitter word. "Must you?"

"I—I must, dear!" he said desperately, his eyes trying wretchedly to avoid hers. "It shan't be long, I promise you; but I must wait just a little longer!"

She paused a moment, still looking into his face. Then, with a sudden light in her eyes, she made a slight movement as though she would have bent his head down that she might murmur in his ear. She stopped herself, however, and there settled down upon her face a look of unutterable sadness. By Julian, in his helpless misery of self-contempt, the gesture had passed utterly unheeded.

"Don't let it be much longer, dear!" she said. "Good night!"

Julian caught at the last word as though it gave him some sort of chance of restoring his writhing self-respect.

"Good night!" he echoed. "Not yet, Clemence! I'm going to see you home, of course!"

But Clemence shook her head.

"No!" she said steadfastly, "no, dear!" Something in her tone, something in the touch she laid upon him, took from him all power of self-assertion, all power of resistance to her will. She drew his head towards her now, kissed him softly on the forehead, and then turned and went away down the street, leaving him alone.

CHAPTER III

"ROMAYNE, at last! By Jove, old man, we thought you were going to throw us over!"

The voice, a young man's voice, struck out, as it were, from an indescribable medley of incongruous sound. The background was formed by the lightest and most melodious dance music, produced solely from stringed instruments; lutes and guitars seemed to predominate, and the result had a character and rhythm of its own which was essentially graceful, picturesque, and Italian; against the background, a high-pitched discord compounded of every imaginable key, there clashed a very Babel of tongues—the eminently unmusical voice of modern society, with all its faults of modulation and pronunciation, blended into a whole full of a character absolutely incompatible with the old-time southern harmonies with which it mingled.

The speaker's figure, as he stopped suddenly in a hurried passage across the room, stood out from a blaze of colour, light, and gorgeousness of every description, which fell without pause or cessation into ever fresh combination, as the beautifully dressed crowd moved to and fro in its magnificent setting. And the spectacle presented to the eye was as curiously jarring, as strikingly suggestive of the ludicrous inconsistencies of dreamland, as were the sounds that saluted the ear. There was hardly a man or woman to be seen whose dress was not as faithful a copy of the costume prevalent among the Florentine nobles under the magnificent rule of the Medici as time and money could make it. There was not a false note in the surroundings; money had been poured out like water in order that a perfect reproduction of an old Florentine palace might be achieved; and as far as art could go nothing was left to be desired. The fault lay with nature. The old Italians doubtless had their own mannerisms, possibly their own vulgarities, of carriage, gesture, and general demeanour; but theirs were not the mannerisms and vulgarities of modern "smart" society.

The young man who had greeted Julian exemplified in his own person all the preposterous incongruity of the whole. His dress was a marvel of correctness to the minutest detail. Its wearer's face was of the heavy, inanimate, bull-dog type; his movement as he shook hands with Julian was an exaggerated specimen of the approved affectation of the moment; his speech was clipped and drawled after the most approved model among "mashers." He was the son of the house, and there was a kind of slow excitement about his manner, struggling with a nonchalant carelessness which he evidently wished to present to the world as his mental attitude of the moment. There was a note of excitement also in the medley of voices about him. The "affair" was "a huge go"—as the young man himself would have expressed it. And neither he nor any one of his father's guests was troubled for one instant by any sense of the ludicrousness of the effect produced.

Julian had that instant entered the room and had paused on the threshold. There is perhaps no type of costume more picturesque in its magnificence than that of the Italian noble of the Middle Ages—this is perhaps the reason why it has been so extensively vulgarised—and Julian's dress was an admirable specimen of its kind, rich, graceful, and becoming. There was a subtle difference between his bearing and that of his host, though Julian's demeanour, too, was modern to the finest shade. He wore the dress well, with none of the other man's awkwardness, but on the contrary with an absolute ease and unconsciousness which implied a certain excited tension of nerve. His face was colourless and very hard; but upon the hardness there was a mask of animation and gaiety which was all-sufficient for the present occasion.

"I'm awfully sorry, dear boy!" he said now, lightly and eagerly, and with an exaggerated gesture of deprecation. "It's horribly late, I know! Give you my word I couldn't help it! By Jove, what a magnificent thing you've made of this!"

The other glanced round with a satisfaction which he tried in vain to repress.

"Not so bad, is it?" he said carelessly. "Only these fellows are such fools, even the best of them; they always blunder if they can." With this wholesale condemnation of the workmen among whom, some fifty years ago, his grandfather might have been found, he screwed his eyeglass into his eye, serenely unconscious of the comic effect produced, for the better contemplation of a pretty girl at the farther end of the room. "Lady Pamela looks awfully fit, doesn't she?" he observed parenthetically; continuing almost in the same breath: "The gardens are the best part, seems to me. Awfully like the real thing, don't you know!"

Julian's only direct answer was an expressive gesture of appreciation and apology.

"Awfully well done!" he said. "Excuse me, dear boy, I see my mother, and she'll want to know why I've not turned up before. I must go and explain."

His companion laughed; the laugh was rather derisive, and the glance he cast on Julian through his eyeglass was stupidly inquisitive and incredulous.

"What a fellow you are, Romayne!" he said. "They ought to put you in a glass case and label you the model son."

Another gay, expressive gesture from Julian.

"Why not?" he said lightly. "We're a model pair, you know."

And the next moment he was threading his way quickly across the room. A sudden movement of the crowd had shown him his mother's figure, and he had realised instinctively that she had seen him. He came up to her with a manner about which there was something indescribably reckless, and made her a low bow of gay and abject apology.

"I beg ten thousand million pardons!" he said. "Language fails to express my feelings."

Mrs. Romayne's dress was not a success—that is to say, it was perfect in itself, and failed only as a setting for its wearer; to deprive her appearance of any possibility of "chic" or "dash" was to deprive it of all its brilliancy. But no unsuitability of colouring or cut in her gown could have been responsible for the look which underlay her smile, as she turned to Julian now and struck a little attitude of mock implacability, with a light, high-pitched laugh.

"Then the conversation must be carried on in dumb show," she said, "for language also fails to express my feelings, sir. What have you to say for yourself?"

Her voice, for all its gaiety, was thin and strained.

"Please, nothing," was the mock-humility answer. "I met a fellow, and he beguiled me. He was just off to America."

He was standing with his hands folded and his eyes cast down, and he did not see—he would not have understood if he had seen—the strange flash in those hard, blue eyes—such a flash as might leap up in the eyes of a woman in the silent endurance of a swift stab of pain.

"A very poor excuse," declared Mrs. Romayne gaily. "No, I don't think I shall forgive you yet. Such unscrupulous desertion must be visited as it deserves. Don't you think so?"

Lord Garstin had come up to them, and the question was addressed to him with a light laugh as she gave him her hand. He nodded pleasantly to Julian as he answered:

"Who has deserted? Not this boy of yours, eh?"

Mrs. Romayne laughed again, and pushed Julian playfully with her fan.

"Oh, I forgot! You don't know his wickedness, of course! Take me away from him, Lord Garstin, do, and I'll confide in you. Gorgeous affair this, isn't it? I wonder what it cost?"

Lord Garstin looked round with a rather lofty smile. There were times when it pleased him to pose as an isolated representative of a bygone age by the traditions of which, in matters of taste and breeding, the present age was utterly condemned.

"Rather too gorgeous to please an old man," he said now with a fine reserve. "These dear good people would be more to my taste, do you know, if they had a little less money. Have you been outside, by-the-bye? It's really not badly done."

Mrs. Romayne turned away with him, laughing and nodding to Julian, and then she stopped and went towards her son again, touching his shoulder lightly.

"Every one isn't so stony-hearted as I am, bad boy," she whispered gaily. "Somebody has actually kept you some dances, I believe, if you apologise properly. Look, there she is."

She made a little gesture with her fan towards the entrance to the dancing-room, from which Maud Pomeroy was just emerging, looking like a picture in a white dress of the simplest form, her long hair loose on her shoulders, and crowned with a wreath of flowers. The dance music had stopped, and the music which still filled the air came from the garden. With that hard recklessness growing stronger on his face, Julian made a slight, graceful gesture towards his mother as though he would have kissed his hand to her in gratitude, turned away, and moved rapidly over to Miss Pomeroy.

More than three hours had gone by since Julian had found himself standing alone gazing stupidly in the direction in which Clemence had disappeared, and how the first two of those hours had passed he hardly knew. He had turned abruptly away and left the little street, to walk mechanically on and on, struggling blindly in a black abyss of self-contempt, in which his love lived only as additional torture.

He had emerged gradually from that abyss, or rather his sense of its surrounding blackness had faded by degrees, as all such acute sensations must. And so completely had that blackness walled him in, and deadened all his outward perceptions, that it was only little by little, and with a dull sense of surprise, that his material surroundings dawned on him again, and he realised that he was standing looking down into the river from the Thames Embankment. His consciousness had come back to that life and world which he believed to constitute the only practical realities; but it had brought with it that which turned all its environment to bitterness and gall. As he stood leaning on the parapet, staring sullenly down, counting the reflection of the lamps in the dark water beneath him in the moody vacancy of reaction, the necessities of his life began to surround him once more; he saw them all as they were, sordid and base, and yet he neither saw nor attempted to see any possibility of self-extrication. The sound of Big Ben as it struck eleven had brought back to his mind the claims upon him of that particular evening.

At eleven o'clock the carriage had been ordered to take Mrs. Romayne and her party to the dance, and a grim, cynical smile touched his set, white lips as he thought of his mother. He had broken loose, temporarily, he told himself bitterly. He must take up his part again and play the farce out.

That he should throw himself into the task with a wild oblivion of all proportion and limitation, was the inevitable result of all that had gone before; of all the perception and all the blindness with which he was racked and baffled.

Miss Pomeroy saw him coming, and turning her face away, she produced a pretty, well-turned comment on the arrangement of the rooms for the benefit of her cavalier. The next instant Julian stood beside her.

"Don't turn your back on me," he implored gaily. "No fellow ever had such hard luck as I've had to-night. Be a great deal kinder to me than I seem to deserve, and forgive me. Please!"

Miss Pomeroy turned her head and looked at him with a serene calm on her pretty face, which seemed to relegate him to a place among inferior objects entirely indifferent to her. Her voice was perhaps a little too indifferent.

"Oh, Mr. Romayne!" she said. "You've actually appeared!"

"I have," he said. "At last! There's a poor fellow I've seen a good deal of—not one of the regular set, you know, but a thoroughly unlucky chap, always in the wars. He's just off to try his luck on the other side of the world, and I met him this evening most awfully blue and lonely—he hasn't a friend in the world. Of course I had to try and cheer him up a bit, and—there, I couldn't leave him, don't you know. I packed him into the mail train at last, and bolted here as fast as wheels could bring me."

Something of the blank serenity of Miss Pomeroy's face gave way. She lifted the feather fan that hung at her girdle and began to ruffle the feathers lightly against her other hand with lowered eyelids.

"I don't think I should have troubled to hurry as it was so late!" she said, and there was a touch of reproach and resentment in her voice. Her cavalier had drifted away by this time, and in the midst of the constantly moving stream of people she and Julian were practically alone. Julian answered her quickly with eager significance.

"You would—in my place!" he said. "You would if you had had the hope of even one of the dances to which you had been looking forward—well, I won't say how, or for how long. Was it altogether a vain hope? Am I quite too late?"

"You are very late!" was the answer; but the tone was distant and indifferent no longer; and as the sound of the violins rose softly and invitingly once more from the other room a quick question from Julian received a soft affirmative in reply, and he led her triumphantly towards the music.

The room was not too full. The garden, the supper, the "show"—as the guests called it amongst themselves—as a whole, prevented any overcrowding in the dancing-room. But dancing among such cunningly arranged accessories was by no means a commonplace business. The unfamiliar picturesqueness of the room, with its softly scented air, the wonderful effects of colour and light, and above all a certain wild passion and sweetness about the music, was not wholly without effect even on the jaded, torpid receptivity of men and women of the world.

Even Miss Pomeroy's calm was apparently not wholly proof against the intoxication; by the time the music died away there was a bright colour on her cheeks, and a bright light in her eyes. On Julian the atmosphere and the music had had much the same effect as an excessive quantity of champagne might have had. His pale face had flushed hotly, and his eyes were glittering with excitement.

He had become aware during their last turn round the room that his mother was standing in the doorway watching them, this time with Loring in attendance; and with a feverish flash of callous defiance he so guided their movements that they came to a standstill finally close before her.

"Congratulate us!" he cried gaily, "we've broken the record! And congratulate me individually, for I've had the most awfully glorious dance of my life! Hullo, Loring, old man!"

"I'll congratulate you both," was Mrs. Romayne's ready answer, as Loring nodded. "You both look as if you had had a good time. Wonderful show, isn't it? It isn't possible to say what it must have cost. Something appalling, of course. Maud, dear, have you come across Claudia Eden? Over there, don't you see? Isn't it outrageous?"

"By Jove!" ejaculated Julian lightly, looking in the direction indicated by a slight movement of his mother's fan, as Miss Pomeroy uttered an exclamation of pretty amazement. Conspicuous against all the magnificence about her was a girl in a kind of burlesque of an Italian contadina dress of the period, with very short skirts, very low-cut bodice, very exaggerated head-dress. She was talking and laughing with a little crowd of men; her manner was as pronounced and as unrefined as her dress; but there was about her that absolutely unconscious and impenetrable self-possession and self-assurance which stamped her as being by birth that which she was certainly not in appearance—a lady, and a very highly born lady.

"She would do anything to make a sensation," murmured Miss Pomeroy, contemplating her critically.

"But have you two seen the gardens?" went on Mrs. Romayne gaily. "No? Then you must simply go instantly. The most marvellous thing I ever saw! Go along at once."

With a laugh Julian turned to Miss Pomeroy. "We must do as we are bidden, of course," he said. "Will it bore you frightfully?"

A smile and the slightest possible shrug of the shoulders constituted Miss Pomeroy's answer, and they were turning away together, followed by a keen glance from Loring, when the girl in the contadina dress, passing close to them with her somewhat noisy court, intercepted their passing.

"'Evening, Maud," she said in a loud, good-natured voice, which might have been delicate and high-bred if fashion had not demanded other characteristics. "Hullo, Mr. Romayne! Like my frock, Maud?"

Miss Pomeroy murmured something gracefully inaudible, and Mrs. Romayne said, with a smile:

"Most original, Lady Claudia."

A restless gleam had come into Mrs. Romayne's eyes at the momentary pause, but there was a certain satisfaction, too, in her smile as the two girls stood face to face. Maud Pomeroy certainly never appeared to greater advantage than in contrast with a pronounced type of the modern society girl. The juxtaposition seemed to bring into strong relief everything about her appearance and demeanour which was dainty, gentle, and sweet, and to throw into shade all her more negative charm. Her voice, now, perfectly modulated and absolutely even, made the other girl seem "quite too vulgar," as Mrs. Romayne said to herself. She echoed Mrs. Romayne's words, and added:

"How came you to think of it?"

"I thought it would score," returned the other, with a laugh. "I can't stand these people, don't you know! I thought of getting a whole lot of us to do it; it would have been no end of a joke! Then I thought that I'd keep it to myself. Ta-ta!"

And with a rough, ungraceful gesture of farewell she passed on.

"Lady Claudia's hostess would strangle her, cheerfully, with her own hands," remarked Loring placidly.

Mrs. Romayne laughed.

"So would a great many other people," she said. "But come, you two be off and see these gardens."

Julian and Miss Pomeroy moved away as if with one consent, and Mrs. Romayne watched them as they went with such a strange intentness in her face, that she looked for the moment as though her consciousness were actually leaving her to follow the two on whom her eyes were fixed.

The idea of the whole entertainment had originated, so people said, in the fact that its giver had spent enormous sums of money in the course of the past three years on the transformation of his grounds into an Italian garden, and the scene from the terrace, as Julian and Miss Pomeroy stepped out on to it, was indeed extraordinarily effective. There was no moon, and thousands of coloured lamps, skilfully disposed, shed a picturesque, uncertain light, under which the long ilex-shaded alleys, the box hedges, the fountains, and the statues produced an illusion which was almost perfect.

"By Jove!" exclaimed Julian in the same strained, excited voice. "Capital, isn't it? It must be almost worth while to live away here in the wilds of Fulham to have a place capable of being turned into a show like this. Don't you think so?"

Miss Pomeroy did not answer immediately. Apparently, the excitement created by their dance had rather strengthened than diminished during the interval, and she was playing almost nervously with her fan. Miss Pomeroy was not a nervous person as a rule.

"I don't know," she said vaguely. "Yes, it's very pretty, isn't it? But I don't think I should much care to have a big place, do you know. I don't think places make much difference."

Her voice was low, and very prettily modulated, and Julian threw a quick sideways glance at her. Except for a flush, and a certain look in her eyes which he could not see, her face was as demure and placid as ever.

"Don't you?" he said. "You are right, of course, and I am wrong. I can imagine circumstances under which all this would be a howling wilderness to me."

He looked at her very differently this time, with his eyes recklessly eloquent. She dropped her own eyes quickly, and said softly:

"Can you?"

They had strolled down the steps as they talked, and at their right hand a picturesque little alley, with a vista of fountain and statue against a grove of ilex-trees, led away from the more open space in front of the house. Down this alley, secluded and apparently deserted, Miss Pomeroy turned, as if unconsciously, before she spoke again. Julian followed her lead with an ugly smile on his face.

Then she said in the same pretty, low voice:

"Tell me what circumstances?"

Julian laughed, and his laugh might well have been construed as a sign of extreme nervousness and agitation.

"I think not!" he said. "I might make you angry."

"You would not make me angry!"

They came to the end of the alley as she spoke; it opened out on a quaint little corner containing a fish-pond surrounded by a stone balustrade, the fountain in the middle sparkling and dancing in the gleam of the artificial moonlight which had been arranged here and there about the grounds to give the finishing touch to sundry "bits." Into this moonlight Maud Pomeroy stepped, and stood leaning gracefully over the balustrade gazing down into the water, as she said in a voice just low and hesitating enough to be perfectly distinct:

"Mr. Romayne, will you tell me—did you think me very angry when you came to-night?"

"I hope you are not angry now, at least!" was the answer, spoken with eager anxiety. "But I would rather think you had been angry than believe that you were quite indifferent as to whether I came or not!"

"I am not—indifferent!" Maud Pomeroy paused. There was no colour at all in her cheeks now, and her lips were drawn together in a hard, thin line such as no one had ever seen on her face before. There was a dead silence. A sudden stillness had come over Julian's figure as he stood also leaning against the balustrade, but with his back to the water. His hand was clenched fiercely against the stone.

"I have no right to be angry with you," Maud Pomeroy went on; her voice was thin and hard as if its steadiness was the result of deliberate effort. "I have no rights at all. If I had———" She let her voice die away again with deliberate intention.

The silence that followed had something ghastly in it. At last, with his face as white as death, and keeping his eyes fixed steadily before him, Julian moved.

"You will catch cold, I'm afraid!" he said, a little hoarsely. "Shall we go in?"

Without a single word Miss Pomeroy moved also and retraced her steps up the alley. For one moment, and for one moment only, her face was no longer that of a gentle and amiable girl, but of a spiteful and vindictive woman.

CHAPTER IV

MORE than one of the people who had talked to Mrs. Romayne in the interval had been vaguely aware of a certain incontrollable preoccupation behind her manner; though the intense, suppressed excitement in which that preoccupation originated passed undetected. Her restless eyes fastened upon Miss Pomeroy and Julian on the very instant of their reappearance in the room, and as they came towards her that excitement leapt up suddenly and lit up her whole face with a wild flash of hope and anticipation. They drew nearer and it died down again even more suddenly than it had sprung up; and in its passing it seemed to have aged her face curiously, and to have left upon it a stamp of heart-sick disappointment, touched with a creeping anxiety. Miss Pomeroy was pale, and her usual still placidity seemed to be accentuated into absolute stupidity. Julian's face was quite colourless, and beneath the travesty of his usual manner which he assumed in speaking to his mother, there was an indefinable expression which made him look ten years older and twenty years harder and more bitter.

Scruples on his part as to crushing their dress prevented his going home with them. He would follow in a hansom, he said. But before he arrived Miss Pomeroy had said good night to Mrs. Romayne with a neatly-turned and quite meaningless expression of the pleasure the evening had given her, and had retired to her room. Mrs. Romayne, looking haggard and worn, lingered until Julian came in, and went out to meet him.

"Good night, mother," he said, and went straight upstairs without pausing.

It was many, many years since he had left her at night without a kiss; and as Mrs. Romayne went slowly up to her room through the silent house, she stumbled once or twice as though her wide, dry eyes hardly saw the stairs before her.

That creeping anxiety had gained ground greatly in her face the next morning when she came down at about half-past ten, to learn from the servant that "Mr. Julian" had already breakfasted and had gone to the Temple. Even more pathetic than the anxiety itself was the courage that battled against it; that strove so hard to become confidence as she led—and, indeed, sustained— the conversation, as she and Miss Pomeroy, who was late in putting in an appearance, breakfasted together. She talked lightly and gaily of Julian's defection on this, their visitor's last morning; she deplored the fact that it was indeed the last morning, talking of various half-formed schemes for such constant meetings as would be practically a continuance of the intimate association of the past fortnight. But of response she obtained little or none. An access of conventionality, demureness, and insipidity seemed to be inspiring Miss Pomeroy; an access characterised by a certain absolute obstinacy of colourlessness. She had no opinions, no sentiments of any sort or kind to offer; her expressions of regret at leaving were as unmeaning as they were correct. Mrs. Romayne's plans seemed to wither under her little non-committal smile and comment; and she took her irreproachable leave an hour later with a vaguely expressed hope that they might meet "somewhere," and apparently without hearing Mrs. Romayne's parting allusion to Julian.

Each one of the days that followed seemed to leave upon Mrs. Romayne's face some such effect as might have been produced upon a marble counterpart of that face by the delicate application of a sharp modelling tool. Every feature became a little sharper; every line a little deeper, a little harder. Nobody noticed the fact, and nobody could have traced it to its source had they done so. But there were times when she was alone; times when that chisel under which she grew more haggard every day revealed itself as heart-sick, gnawing anxiety.

For three or four days Miss Pomeroy's hope that they might meet "somewhere" remained unfulfilled; and Mrs. Romayne made little jokes at what she assumed to be Julian's disconsolate condition; jokes which, taken in conjunction with the look in her eyes as she spoke them, were almost ghastly. Then the meeting took place at a party from which, as it appeared, Miss Pomeroy and her mother were just departing; so that a few words of greeting on either side was all that passed.

Mrs. Pomeroy and her daughter called on Mrs. Romayne a day or two later. It was Mrs. Romayne's "day," of course; the room was very full, and as Mrs. Pomeroy said, with an expression as near apprehension as was compatible with her placidity in the eyes which kept turning to her daughter's demure face: "Wednesday is such a popular day, and we've really dozens of calls to pay, haven't we, Maud?" Consequently they stayed barely ten minutes, and exchanged half-a-dozen sentences with their hostess. But short and formal as the call was, it was supplemented by no more intimate intercourse. They met, of course, nearly every day. That is to say, Mrs. Romayne, as she went about indefatigably from party to party, caught constant glimpses of Miss Pomeroy and her mother just arriving as she left, just leaving as she arrived, just going to supper, to tea, to fulfil some social duty or other which made it impossible that more than a word or two should pass. When Mrs. Romayne pressed Miss Pomeroy, with sprightly reproaches, to come and see her, she was met invariably with unmeaning smiles, and vague words about engagements, which, gentle as they sounded, proved as little capable of manipulation as a stone. Once or twice after such a meeting, Mrs. Romayne's jokes at Julian's expense, as she told him of them airily afterwards—Julian and Miss Pomeroy never seemed to meet now—took the form of hints and innuendoes as to whether he was not at the bottom of "the mystery," as she called it; and whether he could not perhaps sweep it away. There was a terrible contrast between the casual gaiety with which such hints were dropped by her, and the something which lay behind; something which gave her voice a strange, unnatural ring, and cut her words off almost before they had any meaning; something the name of which, as it lurked in the hard, bright eyes which never met Julian's, was nervous fear.

Such hints were always met and turned by Julian as lightly as they were uttered.

Before a fortnight had passed since Miss Pomeroy's departure, Mrs. Romayne had acquired a habit of giving one quick, almost furtive, glance round any room she entered in which people were assembled, and that look was particularly eager and intent as she entered a drawing-room to fulfil an engagement for a luncheon-party one day at the beginning of the third week. A luncheon is by no means a bad opportunity for a "quiet chat." She did not see the figures she was in search of, though no one could have detected that fact from her expression. Nor could any one have interpreted the sudden exclamation of surprise she uttered.

"Why, it's Dennis Falconer!" she said prettily. "I had no idea you were in town."

It was Dennis Falconer; not a little altered by the past eight months, and altered for the better. Six months earlier he had disappeared from the ken of his society acquaintances; disappeared quietly, almost imperceptibly. By-and-by, when his absence began to be commented upon, rumour had whispered it abroad that he was "laid up or something." The fact, so lightly stated and equally lightly commented on, had meant for Falconer a realisation of the possibilities hinted at by his doctor early in November. He had passed from the dreariness of unoccupied and somewhat lonely club life into the infinitely heavier dreariness of a solitary sick-room.

Within his own limits and on his own lines Dennis Falconer was a strong man. With his dark hour absolutely upon him he braced himself to meet it with stern dignity; and he endured four months of physical suffering and mental tedium—from which that suffering, weary and unremitting as it was, was seldom acute enough to relieve him—with uncomplaining fortitude. He was quite alone. Circumstances had occurred to detain Dr. Aston in India, and his solitude was not realised by any of his club acquaintances. It was a period on which, in after life, he never willingly looked back; a dark hour, in truth. But it was lived through at last, and as it passed away it gave place to a clear and steady light, in which the shadows which had preceded it had vanished. Severe as had been the means, the end was amply attained. He emerged from his sick-room in such perfect physical health as he had not known for years. All the disabilities under which he had laboured during the preceding summer were removed, and in every nerve and muscle he was conscious of vigorous life. In May he had received his doctor's permission to return to his work, and he was in London now to arrange the preliminaries of an expedition with which he hoped to leave England early in the autumn.

The physical change in him was conspicuous as he stepped forward to return Mrs. Romayne's greeting. He looked ten years younger than he had been wont to look; the worn look of endurance had gone, and there was an air of strength and power about him which was very noticeable. Hardly less striking was the change in his expression. Much of the grim austerity of his demeanour during the previous summer had originated in the painful depression consequent on his state of health; much also in his realisation of his position as a man laid aside and solacing himself as best he might. The gravity and reserve of his expression remained, but the heaviness had disappeared completely.

His manner to Mrs. Romayne, as he shook the hand she held out to him, was significant of the lighter and more tolerant point of view from which his own lighter prospects unconsciously led him to contemplate his fellow-creatures. It was neither expansive nor friendly, but it lacked that undercurrent of stiff condemnation which had previously characterised it.

"I have intended to call on you," he said with grave directness. "I am sorry to appear negligent. But my time is no longer at my own disposal."

Mrs. Romayne put aside the claim on his time which he imputed to her with a quick gesture and a laugh.

"You are quite recovered, I hope?" she said easily. "Tiresome business, convalescence, isn't it?"

"I am quite recovered, I am thankful to say," responded Falconer; he was so keenly conscious of all that the words meant for him that he was insensible even to the jarring effect her manner had always had for him. "I hope before very long to be at work again. Indeed, I am practically at work now."

"Yes?" said Mrs. Romayne prettily. "Are you thinking of going abroad again?"

"I am going out to Africa. I shall hardly be in England again for another five years."

Mrs. Romayne had been looking vaguely about the room, evidently bestowing a modicum of her attention only on Falconer. But as he spoke the last words the slightest possible start passed through her frame and her wandering eyes suddenly ceased to wander. There was a moment's pause, and then she turned them on Falconer's face.

"Really? And when do you go?"

There was something rather odd beneath the carelessness of her voice, and her eyes, as she fixed them on Falconer's, were odd too.

"I hope to leave England early in October."

Mrs. Romayne made no reply. Her face suggested curiously that the actual exigencies of the situation had faded for her, that she was not in the present at all. For the moment there was no trace of that satisfaction and relief which would have been the natural consummation, on such news, of the defiance and distaste so hardly repressed in her manner to her "connexion" during the past year. She looked, apparently unconsciously, into the grave, steady man's face above her, and there was a vague, half-formed expression in her eyes, which might have been a suddenly-stirred sense of loneliness or foreboding.

It was gone again in an instant. And as the man who was to take her in to lunch approached her, she turned from Falconer with the lightest possible "au revoir."

Falconer found himself very well situated at luncheon. A question came up on which his word carried weight, and the discussion which ensued brought home to him that sense of renewed power and standing in the world so grateful to him after his long period of inaction. He was full of grave content and satisfaction, when, after lunch, circumstances threw him again with Mrs. Romayne; and his whole mental attitude was suffused with a dignified kindliness. He began to speak at once with grave, but not unfriendly interest, and as though he were conscious of a certain remissness.

"I am glad to hear of your son! I hope it is quite satisfactory to you?"

Mrs. Romayne had acknowledged his vicinity with a conventional word and smile. Circumstances demanded of her at the moment no active exertion; she was standing aside, as it were, for the instant, and there were tired lines faintly visible about her mouth. They disappeared, however, as if by magic, beneath the hard intentness which leapt into her face as she turned sharply to Falconer on his first words. The movement was apparently involuntary, for she turned away, lifting with elaborate carelessness the long eye-glasses which she had lately adopted, as though to cover the first movement, and said, as she looked through them at something at the other end of the room:

"It's very stupid of me, no doubt, but I must ask you to explain!"

The neutrality of her previous conversation with him had vanished as completely as the strange suggestion with which it had ended had vanished.

The old defiance, apparently entirely uncalled-for, rang in her elaborately indifferent voice.

"Is it so old a story?" said Falconer. "Or is it, perhaps, a mistake?" he added with genuine regret. "I hope not. A sensible marriage is such a safeguard—a covenant with society. I heard of your son's engagement some three weeks ago on what purported to be excellent authority."

"Did you hear the name of the young lady by any chance?"

Mrs. Romayne achieved a harsh little laugh as she spoke.

Falconer glanced round the room and lowered his voice.

"Miss Maud Pomeroy!" he said. "A most desirable wife for him, I should have said!"

Eight months before, under the inexplicable influence of the face and manner of the pale, dignified woman who had faced him so bravely in the little lodging in Camden Town, Dennis Falconer had been almost ready to urge upon Julian Romayne marriage with the girl he was supposed to have ruined. But he would have done so convinced, in the recesses of his heart to which that woman's influence could not penetrate, that such a course must mean ruin to the young man; and in the grim severity of his mental attitude at the time, he would have said that such ruin was the just and righteous consequence of the young man's guilt. Clemence's disappearance had frustrated the possibility of any such action on his part; time and the pressing actualities of his own life had obliterated the impression made on him; and the whole affair had gradually faded into the past. Insensibly to himself he looked upon it now, conventionally enough, as one of those dark episodes which are in no way to be obliterated or lightened, but which may and must be overlaid. To that end it seemed to him, in the relaxation of his sterner attitude, a thing so natural as to be necessarily condoned that Julian should marry in his own class and settle down.

A moment's pause followed on his words. Mrs. Romayne was sweeping the room with her eye-glasses. The hand which held them shook a little, and, if the man beside her could have known it, she saw absolutely nothing.

"Maud Pomeroy!" she said at last, and she seemed to be unconscious of that moment's interval of silence. "Ah! Well, to tell you the truth, that is not such an extraordinary report, though it hardly represents the fact—at present. Young people will be young people, you know, and they must be allowed their little wilfulnesses!"

She also had lowered her voice, though it was high-pitched, and her speech was almost exaggeratedly confidential. Influenced by the tone into which they had thus fallen, Falconer said, meaningly and not unkindly:

"You have had to make no more serious allowances, I hope—since?"

With a laugh so light and high as to be painfully out of tune, Mrs. Romayne answered him gaily in the negative. One little peccadillo, she said, was not such a very terrible thing in a young man's record, and she was charmed to say that with that little affair of which they both knew her anxieties on Julian's account had begun and ended. She held out her hand to Falconer as she finished her assurance, parting with him with her brightest air of society friendliness, and as he wished her good-bye, looking down into the trivial vivacity of her face, Falconer felt himself stirred for the first time by a certain touch of pity for her. Coming upon his softer mood and the comparatively friendly nature of their talk, the eager assurance with which she spoke struck him as being not without pathos. He had no confidence in Julian, and it occurred to him vaguely and with a sense of surprise that if the security so superficially founded should prove false, the blow would be somewhat disproportionate to the lightness of the nature on which it must fall. The next instant he recollected how largely her own actions would have contributed to bring about the blow, and he dismissed her sternly from his thoughts as she passed out of the room.

Mrs. Romayne went straight home, though she had numerous calls on her list for the afternoon; her eyes were even desperately bright and defiant; and that same evening Marston Loring received a note asking him to come and see her on the following day.

He found her waiting for him in the drawing-room at the hour she had appointed, and she plunged into the matter in hand with an affectation of spontaneous confidence which was most effective.

She had sent for him in his capacity of fellow-conspirator, she told him; she was in a little perplexity and she was turning to him, as usual—this with a charming smile—to help her. From this prelude she went on to speak of the strange change which had come about in the relations between herself and Julian on the one hand, and the Pomeroys on the other. Loring's keen eyes had detected this change some time since—by this time, indeed, it was being whispered about somewhat freely—but he only listened with grave attention. The upshot of her speech was: did Loring know anything about it? Had Julian said anything? Had he spoken of any quarrel, of any misunderstanding? Had his friend any kind of clue to give her as to his feelings on the subject?

The ease and gaiety of her manner, which strove to give to the whole thing something the air of a joke, was disturbed and broken as she came to the point by a feverishness about which there was nothing gay or light. And some uncertainty as to how far she had gone seemed to pervade her mind and to produce a feeling that some kind of explanation was necessary.

"You see," she said, "it isn't always safe to go to the fountain-head in these little matters! A young man doesn't always care to be questioned by his mother! One might 'give offence,' you know!" Her tone was playful, but her eyes were filled with the nervous fear which lurked in them so often when she and Julian were alone together, and the look on her face as she spoke her last words seemed to give to that fear a definite object. It was the fear of "giving offence" to her son.

Loring put the explanation aside with a smile, but he had no words of enlightenment for her. Julian, he said, had preserved a total silence on the subject.

"I will see what I can do," he said finally, with a smile that cancelled the offensiveness of the intention conveyed of "pumping" his friend. "And we will confer further. Meanwhile, I know you will like to hear that his financial proceedings are prospering exceedingly, and are discretion itself!"

But the further conference, which took place in a day or two, was entirely fruitless as far as its nominal purpose was concerned. Loring did not reveal to Mrs. Romayne the exceeding brevity and decision with which Julian had dealt with any and every attempt to lead the conversation towards the Pomeroys, but he gave her to understand that at present he had nothing to tell her.

One night, about a week later, when she and her son came home in the dawn of the July day from a series of "at homes," Mrs. Romayne, instead of saying good night to Julian at the door of her room, as was her custom, laid her hand suddenly on his arm and drew him just across the threshold. Her face was white to the very lips, and there was a set desperation in it stronger even than the fear with which her eyes were full. Her voice, as she spoke, was breathless and uncertain as though her heart beat with painful rapidity.

"Julian," she said, "what is it that has gone wrong between you and Maud Pomeroy?"

A flash, so quick in the passing that its intense bitterness was not to be detected, passed across Julian's face; it seemed to leave him armed with an expression of determined brightness which defied all emotion or sentiment.

"I don't know that anything has 'gone wrong,' dear," he said lightly.

His mother's hold on his arm tightened desperately.

"I saw what happened to-night in the supper-room," she said. "Won't you"—her voice broke, and there came to it a strangely beseeching note—"won't you tell me what it is?"

Julian's face grew rather set, and he paused a moment. Then he said, still in the same tone:

"It is nothing that I need worry you about, dear."

"Something might be done. If I knew what it was it could be set right, I know."

"No, dear!" The words came from Julian quickly and instantly, and there was a decision and significance behind his light tone now. Her speech had created a necessity, and he rose instinctively to meet it. "I'm awfully sorry to distress you, but I assure you nothing can be done. A girl must be allowed to know her own mind, you know. And a certain little question asked and answered, the only thing left to the fellow is to retire gracefully. I'm awfully sorry you are cut up about it; I was afraid you would be. Never mind, dear. I'm in no particular hurry."

He had gained in fluency and expansiveness of manner as he proceeded; the expedient had only occurred to him on the spur of the moment; and as he finished he bent down and kissed her lightly on the forehead.

"Good night," he said. "Sleep as well as I intend to do."

He left her with a nod and a smile, shutting the door behind him, and Mrs. Romayne stood for a moment motionless, as she had received his kiss, staring at the door through which he had disappeared. Then she began to rub her hands feebly against one another as though a great cold had seized her. She was trembling from head to foot.

"Failed!"

She spoke the word half aloud in a low, shivering tone, which gave to its isolated utterance a strangely weird effect.

CHAPTER V

MARSTON Loring was sitting at his writing-table, writing with an intentness which harmonised oddly with the suggestion of his evening dress—correct and up-to-date in the minutest particular. He had come rapidly out from the inner room two or three minutes before, evidently acting upon a recently-formed determination; and he was writing now swiftly and decisively. But there was nothing of rashness or impulsiveness about his face or manner as he wrote; they were even keener, more calculating and cynical than usual. He finished his note, directed it with the same decision, pushed it aside, and, taking up an open letter which had been lying before him as he wrote, leant back in his chair, and began to re-read it. The note, on which the ink was scarcely dry, was addressed to a broker in the City. The letter which he had taken up bore the postmark of a small town in South Africa, and was marked "Private" and "Urgent."

Three days had passed since Julian's explanation to his mother as to his relations with Miss Pomeroy.

Marston Loring had come back from South Africa three months before, with some very excellent machinery ready to his hand for the production of what would materially simplify and embellish his future career—a large fortune. That the machinery was such as a man of honour would have hesitated to put in motion; that the hands which worked it could hardly escape unstained, affected him not at all. The stains were not such as could be pointed at; it was hardly likely that they would be detected. Certain fellow mechanics were necessary to the proceedings; one of these he had found in Ramsay; the other he had created, so to speak, in Julian Romayne.

The first noticeable production of that machinery had been that first decisive rise in "Welcomes" at the end of June; and since that time it had been worked—mainly by the master-mechanics, Ramsay and Loring—with unceasing skill, energy, and unscrupulousness. Various causes had co-operated to prevent such a speedy consummation as Loring had anticipated when he told Julian that the inside of a month would see the end of the proceedings. The month had gone by, and the shares, though they were now worth ten times as much as had been paid for them by the three in whose hands they lay, had not yet touched the highest value to which it was proposed to raise them—to which they were rising, as a matter of fact, with ever-increasing rapidity. And yet, notwithstanding the apparent certainty that in another week his shares would have materially increased in value, the note which Loring had just written contained instructions for the disposal of all his interest in the Welcome Diamond Mining Company, without fail, on the following day.

A very small stone will put out of gear the most skilfully constructed and reliable machine. A very small modicum of fact will reduce the most skilful and elaborate fiction to its elements. The letter which Loring was studying now with knit brows and compressed lips brought him private information, which he knew might be public property twenty-four hours later, to the effect that the Welcome Diamond Mine was under water. As soon as that fact was generally made known, shares in the Company would be practically worthless.

He folded the letter and sat for a moment tapping it meditatively against the table. He was thinking deeply; not now about the actual contents of the letter, but of a question which they had raised in his mind; a question interwoven and complicated with other carefully-laid plans. Finally he threw the letter down on the table with a movement of sudden resolution.

"I must!" he said to himself. "It won't do to risk a row."

He glanced hastily at his watch, and then drew out a sheet of note-paper and wrote rapidly:

"Dear Julian,

"Be here to-morrow at ten sharp. Don't fail.

"Yours,

"Marston Loring."

He directed the letter, and then rose quickly, took up the hat and light overcoat lying on a chair near him, and went out with the letter in his hand. At the porter's lodge he stopped. "Get this sent by hand this evening," he said, giving the man the letter addressed to Julian. The other letter he posted himself as he passed along the Strand.

He was on his way to dine in Curzon Street, and among his subsequent engagements for the evening the Academy soirée occupied a prominent place.

It was nearly twelve o'clock when he arrived at Burlington House, and the vestibule and staircase were alike crowded with people going up and coming down; smiling, nodding, and generally obstructing the way, with a bland oblivion of any but their own individual rights to a passage.

At the foot of the stairs Loring was seized upon and absorbed in a portentous obstruction, of which the centre figure was Mrs. Halse, a truly electrifying figure in a painfully fashionable evening "frock" of a brilliant green.

"I was just looking for a man," she said, in her usual strident tones. "They get such an extraordinary lot of people together here that picking out any one one knows is like looking for a needle in a bundle of hay. I suppose nobody ever did look for a needle in a bundle of hay, by-the-bye. Mr. Halse isn't here, of course"—Mr. Halse was seldom known to appear in public, and when he did so, his meek presence was obviously entirely devoid of interest for his wife—"and I'm looking after Hilda Compton; her husband's coming to fetch her, but he doesn't care about her going about alone. Quite right, too, I tell him," she added, with a laugh. "But of course it won't last."

Hilda Compton, a three months' bride, was standing by looking like a Hilda Newton who had been born and bred in the centre of London society, daring in dress, self-possessed in manner, audaciously pretty in face.

She echoed Mrs. Halse's laugh, and the latter went on, to Loring:

"You can come upstairs with us. It's such a bore not to have a man!" and turning, led the way.

That characteristic feature in her vociferous personality—Mrs. Halse's hobbies—had become crystallised to a great extent since Hilda Newton's engagement and marriage into a passion for matrimonial affairs; not necessarily for match-making; match-marring was quite as keen an interest with her.

The comments with which she beguiled their way into the first room were mainly called forth by the young men and maidens of her acquaintance who happened to catch her eye, and whom she suspected of mutual likings or loathings. They had drifted halfway across the room without coming within speaking distance of any one they knew, when Mrs. Halse broke off in an energetically-whispered account of a certain pretty young woman's partiality for—according to Mrs. Halse—an unresponsive young man, and exclaimed suddenly:

"That's Maud Pomeroy over there, isn't it? It's my belief that she wears those ridiculous white dresses so that people may have something to remember her by. There's nothing in her face, that's certain!"

Loring glanced through the doorway into the other room, to where Miss Pomeroy, in white silk, was smiling very prettily upon a young man who was obviously, if his countenance was to be relied upon, making inane remarks to her. He was a very rich young man, and he had lately succeeded to a title. Loring smiled rather enigmatically.

"It is surely impossible to associate two such dissimilar ideas as artifice and Miss Pomeroy—oil and water, you know."

"Milk and water, you mean!" put in Mrs. Compton, with a laugh.

Mrs. Halse responded to the little witticism with obstreperous hilarity, and then turned suddenly and confidentially to Loring, and spoke in an eager semi-whisper:

"Now, perhaps you can tell me," she said; "nobody who knows her seems to have been able to pick up anything—not that she has any intimate friends, that kind of girl never has. But you know him, and men gossip much more than women, when all's said and done. Has she behaved infamously to him, or has he behaved infamously to her?"

"Has who behaved infamously to whom?" said Loring, smiling.

Mrs. Halse unfurled her fan, and began to waft it vigorously and excitedly to and fro.

"You do know something about it!" she exclaimed. "Hilda, he wouldn't fence like that unless he knew something. But you're not going to get out of it like that," she continued, addressing herself again to Loring. "I'll tell you plainly of whom I am talking, and you'll tell me plainly what has happened. Maud Pomeroy is the she, and young Romayne is the he. Now, then."

"I give you my word that I know nothing about it."

"I don't believe you," was the answer, given with uncompromising vigour and directness. "Good heavens! Somebody must know something about it. A month ago the Romaynes and the Pomeroys were never apart. You couldn't go into a room without seeing him making eyes at her, and her simpering up at him, and their respective mammas exchanging confidences in corners. I was within an ace of congratulating them all round heaps of times. I lived with my mouth open to do it, so to speak; they all seemed so keen about it, it was evidently a matter for fervent congratulation. Though why Mrs. Pomeroy should have cared about it I can't think!" this parenthetically. "He won't have anything of his own while his mother lives. I suppose Maud fancied him! It's my belief that that poor woman daren't call her soul her own where Miss Maud is concerned!"

Mrs. Halse paused, but only for the purpose of taking breath. That very necessary process being accomplished, she continued her summary of the position:

"Then she goes to stay with prospective mamma-in-law, and we all stand on tip-toe and hold our breath. She spends a fortnight there, and the next thing we know is that the whole affair is apparently off! Off, if you please! No more making of eyes, no more simperings, no more confidences. And no explanation of any sort or kind. Mr. Loring, I cannot stand it, and I insist on knowing what you know."

"Mrs. Halse, you do know what I know—that is—nothing."

If a large and smart lady could by any possibility permit herself to stamp a large and heavy foot in the midst of a crowded and fashionable assembly, Mrs. Halse stamped hers at that moment. She gazed for an instant into Loring's imperturbable face, and then, becoming convinced of his sincerity, she turned to Mrs. Compton with a gesture of despair.

"Hilda!" she said, "if somebody doesn't find out something soon, I shall die of suspense!"

As it seemed not improbable from her demeanour at the moment that she would obviate the chances of such a calamity by hurling herself upon one of the objects of her interest and wresting a solution of the mystery from him or her by main force, it was perhaps as well that at that moment a temporary distraction presented itself in the shape of a popular actor. Mrs. Halse was very fond of popular actors; they had been a hobby with her at one time. And in the movement and breaking up of the group which ensued, Loring drifted quietly away.

He had made his way gradually into the big room, when he suddenly quickened his steps and began to thread his way skilfully and rapidly through the crowd. Mrs. Romayne was standing on the opposite side of the room, smiling an invitation to him to come and speak to her.

Mrs. Romayne had not been looking her best lately. Somehow the piquant style and daring colour which she affected hardly suited her as they had been wont to do. To-night there was a tired look upon her face which seemed to reveal some recently-traced lines about her mouth; lines of intense and almost dogged determination; and to her sparkling eyes, if she allowed them a moment's repose, there came a haggard look, which had seemed for the last three days to lie only just beneath the surface. But these were subtle, hardly perceptible points, and for the rest she remained a noticeably attractive woman of the most pronounced artificial type.

"Where's the boy?" said Loring easily, when they had shaken hands. "Is he here?"

Mrs. Romayne shook her head and laughed.

"No!" she said. "He rather bars the soirée. A mistake, I think. One must take it for what it is, of course; an omnium-gatherum of a perfectly preposterous nature; looked at from that point of view it's not unfunny! Do look at that girl over there! She thinks her garment is a revelation to all beholders!"

"So it is," returned Loring drily.

Mrs. Romayne laughed, and dropped the glasses with which she had been coolly surveying the garment in question.

"That was rather obvious, wasn't it?" she said gaily. "By-the-bye, did you want to see Julian?"

There was a moment's pause after Loring had replied, pleasantly enough, in the negative, and then Mrs. Romayne looked up at him suddenly, and said:

"It's frightfully hot in here, don't you think? Suppose we try one of the less popular rooms?" She stopped a moment, and then added with her most artificial laugh: "Of course, you gather from that that I'm going to victimise you again? Yes; I do want a little quiet talk with you. Who'd be a conspirator?"

There was nothing of the unwilling victim, at least, in Loring's tone or manner as he deprecated her words. Nor was there either reluctance or tedium in his face as he followed her through the room. On the contrary, it was almost lighted up by an expression of sudden purpose.

Mrs. Romayne led the way to the almost deserted miniature room, and they began to walk slowly up and down, to all intents and purposes alone together. There seemed to be no particular point to Mrs. Romayne's desire for a private conference with her fellow-conspirator. She talked about Julian; talked about him carelessly, artificially, but with a persistence which only another mother could have understood; slipping in little questions now and then on all sorts of details connected with that business side of a man's life, as to which, she said, "women are always so in the dark;" and reverting again and again to her satisfaction and reliance in his mentor.

"It's rather absurd to quote those ridiculous old proverbs," she said at last, laughing affectedly, "but isn't there one, or a fable, or something, about a duck whose chickens—no, a hen whose chickens, it would be, wouldn't it?—would take to the water, and agitated her awfully because she couldn't go after them? That's exactly what I feel like, I assure you. And I look upon you as an exceptionally sensible water-bird who is also at home on the land—a kind of connecting link. Humiliating similes, aren't they?"

Loring smiled in answer to her laugh. But his tone as he answered her was rather grave.

"Not by any means humiliating as far as I am concerned," he said; "for you assume a certain amount of sympathy between yourself and me. May I tell you what a pleasure that idea gives me?"

He spoke slowly and deliberately, and Mrs. Romayne started slightly. She glanced up at his face for an instant, unfurling her fan, and using it gently, as though the movement were an outlet for some sort of faint agitation. Loring was not looking at her, his eyes were fixed for the moment on the opposite wall, and his profile told her nothing. There was a hardly perceptible pause, and then he went on, with an admirable mixture of deference, admiration—the depth of which seemed the greater in that it was rather suggested than expressed—and the practical confidence of a man of the world.

"Don't think that I am underrating Julian," he said, "or that my regard for him, personally, is anything but a very warm and sincere affair, when I tell you that it is a long time now since Julian has figured in my thoughts as anything but his mother's son. Because he is his mother's son there are very few things I would not do for him, very little trouble I would not take for him."

He hardly paused. Mrs. Romayne, rather, broke in on his speech with a high-pitched laugh.

"That's very kind and flattering," she said, and there was something astonishingly hasty and nervous in the way she spoke.

"I hope it doesn't come upon you quite as a surprise," answered Loring, with the slightest suggestion of a cynical smile unseen by Mrs. Romayne. "I hope it doesn't need any words of mine to show you what I have tried to show you in more practical ways. You have honoured me with a great deal of confidence, and you have honoured me still further by putting it in my power to be of some slight service to you. Will you not give me still further powers in that direction? Will you not make our interests practically one by becoming my wife?"

He turned to her as he finished, and in spite of the admirable composure and deference with which he had spoken, his eyes were very eager and elated, almost as though with anticipated triumph.

Mrs. Romayne met his eyes, and stood for a moment gazing into them speechless and motionless, as though the blank astonishment written on every line of her face had absolutely paralysed her.

"Mr. Loring!" she said at last, and there was an almost bewildered remonstrance in her low, astonished tone. "My dear Mr. Loring!"

"One moment," he interposed quickly. "Of course, I don't ask you to look upon it as anything but a question of expediency and mutual goodwill and esteem. We are both of us very well aware that London is not Arcadia! You won't consider it brutal frankness on my part, I'm sure, if I tell you that from a financial point of view our positions are not unequal. I have been exceptionally fortunate lately, and I can offer you an income of about five thousand a year. And if a man's assistance and support counts for something in your life, as I hope it may——"

Mrs. Romayne interrupted him. With all the tact and practicality of a woman of the world, she had mastered her amazement and was mistress of the situation. She spoke kindly and composedly, with just that touch of delicate concern which the occasion demanded.

"Don't say any more, please; it is really quite impossible."

A sudden flash of surprise passed across Marston Loring's face, and he paused a moment, his keen eyes fixed scrutinisingly on her face. He was trying to detect there some signs of that coquetry or affectation of reluctance which he believed must surely underlie her words. His scrutiny failed to detect anything of the kind, however, and an unpleasant glitter came into his eyes.

"Impossible is a rather curt word," he said. "May I ask you to amplify it?"

He saw the colour rise beneath her paint as she answered:

"I have not the faintest intention of marrying, in the first place. And even if there were not innumerable other reasons against what you propose, I'm afraid I have no fancy for making myself ridiculous! Oh, of course I am well aware"—she laughed a little—"that in my capacity of silly old mother I am as ridiculous as any woman need be! But really, I cannot add another farcical part to that farcical rôle."

"And that farcical part would be——?" enquired Loring.

"That of the old wife of a young husband," she answered, with artificial mirth. "Mr. Loring, I am really sorrier, if you are indeed disappointed, than I can tell you. If you have thought that I encouraged you—— But that is too utterly preposterous! I have considered you simply as my son's friend—almost my son's contemporary—a young man with an exceptionally wise and reliable head. Certainly not as a young man who would be foolish enough to want to marry a woman old enough to be his mother."

Loring's lips were rather thin, and his eyes glittered dangerously. As she stood looking at him then, with a certain softening excitement about her face, there was no slightest suggestion of age about her; nothing but an admirably developed and preserved maturity. And Loring was a young man in nothing but years.

"That is a mere form of words, if you will pardon my saying so," he said, and his voice was dangerously quiet and controlled. "There is difference between us in years, of course, but that goes for nothing. In experience, in knowledge of the world, if I may say so, the difference between us is practically nil. I am, as you say, your son's friend. But is that a reason for refusing me a larger form of the right which you yourself have pressed upon me, to watch over him and to supplement your care where it must inevitably fall short? For Julian's sake!"

He was confronting her now, looking straight down at her, and as he spoke the last words, all the concern and agitation, partly affected, partly real, with which her face had been moved, vanished before a set expression of unalterable resolution.

"For Julian's sake," she said, in a low, decisive voice, "it is impossible."

He stood for a moment watching her, all the evil of his face standing out in intense relief, and then he made a slight, cold gesture of acquiescence.

"May I take you back into the large room?" he said.

She held out her hand to him with an eager gesture of apology and appeal.

"We are friends still?" she murmured. And the murmur was almost pathetically genuine in its anxiety. "It makes no difference?"

Loring's mouth was not good to look at as he answered in a tone absolutely destitute of expression:

"Certainly not!"

CHAPTER VI

IF evil thoughts and evil passions could have a tangible effect upon the physical atmosphere, the air of Marston Loring's room, an hour later, should have been thick and heavy. He was sitting thrown back in an easy-chair, his evening coat replaced by a smoking jacket, a glass of whisky and seltzer-water close to his hand. There were also cigars on the table, but he was not smoking. He was staring straight before him into vacancy. His face was pale and set with vindictive passion, to the existence of which in his nature the general callousness of his expression gave no clue.

It was many years since Marston Loring had felt as he felt to-night. It was many years since he had been foiled and thwarted—"made a fool of," as he himself would have said; and all that was blackest and worst in the man was roused by the process. His life, ever since he had realised, at the age of twenty-five, that there were prizes in the world which some men obtained and other men failed to obtain, had been ruled by a series of carefully made and elaborately worked out calculations. Everything he had done, and everything he had not done, had been included in one or other of these calculations; carefully designed to meet certain ends, all of which met and culminated in the one great end of existence as he conceived it—material prosperity and position.

He had been, perhaps, as vicious a youth as could have been found in London, and he had not ceased to be vicious as a man. But he so managed his vices that even the reputation which clung to him had contributed to his success. The question of marriage he had discussed with himself on more than one occasion, always solely from the point of view of expediency. And just about the time when Mrs. Romayne made her appearance in London society he had come to the conclusion that, given the right sort of woman, the step might possibly prove advantageous. He had been considerably struck by Mrs. Romayne from the first; she was the kind of woman he greatly admired, and he was well aware that to be on terms of intimacy with such a social power was an excellent thing for a man in his position; a position which, as he was also well aware, was by no means so secure as most people supposed. It was from this point of view that he had cultivated Julian, and, at first, from this point of view only. The idea of Mrs. Romayne as a possible wife occurred to him later. But when it did occur, it developed into active intention with considerable rapidity.

He had looked at the question from every possible point of view, and decided that nothing could suit him better. He had no taste for young women. He admired Mrs. Romayne as much as it was possible to him to admire any one; she was "the kind of woman he could get on with," he told himself. She possessed exceptional advantages in the matter of social standing, and she had money. Her eager cultivation of him during the autumn that followed her first season in town convinced him that with a little trouble she could be brought to forget the disadvantage of his comparative poverty; and he would have proposed to her in the ensuing winter had not his voyage to the Cape prevented. He had come back with the prospect of a fortune of his own. But the fact made no difference to his matrimonial plans. Where there is money more money is always to be desired. Mrs. Romayne's fortune was no longer absolutely necessary to him, but it had not ceased to be desirable, and her other advantages remained intact. She had received him with enthusiasm, she had cultivated him assiduously; she had absolutely led him on, as it seemed to Loring. He, in common with the rest of the world, regarded her relations with her son as the merest pose, and her appeal for his help with Julian had seemed to him simply the most transparent of subterfuges. He had no more doubted that she would accept him than he had doubted his own existence. And now his plans were frustrated, his calculations were falsified, and his very practical and material castles in the air were laid in the dust. He was refused.

He roused himself at last, and the faintest suggestion of a cruel smile curved his thin lips. He lifted the glass by his side, drank off its contents, and then turned out the lamp and went into the inner room.

His face was quite itself the next morning; the scowl and the cruelty had alike disappeared; and it was with an even less cynical smile than usual that he looked up from his morning paper at a few minutes past ten o'clock, as the door opened with a hasty knock, and Julian Romayne appeared.

"Good morning, dear boy!" said Loring pleasantly.

"Morning, old man!" responded Julian.

He was looking rather pale and anxious, and he went on quickly:

"Nothing wrong with 'Welcomes,' I hope?"

Loring smiled again.

"Nothing in the world, as far as I know," he said gaily. "What a nervous fellow you are!"

"What an unreasonable fellow you are!" retorted Julian, the cloud vanishing from his face as if by magic. "What do you mean by dragging a poor wretch down here at this hour in the morning, whether he will or no? What's up?"

It was some legal business, it appeared; and Loring proceeded to go into it with great circumstance. It sounded very important as he put it, but Julian took his leave, declaring gaily that he "didn't see where the urgency came in."

"You're such an abominably hard-working fellow!" he said lightly.

"Perhaps!" returned Loring. "It's not such a bad principle, and it's an excellent character to have, let me tell you. By-the-bye, Julian," he continued, as the young man turned away with a laugh, and laid his hand on the door, "how would you like to have a few more Welcomes?"

He rose as he spoke, and stood leaning against the mantelpiece with his back to the empty grate, confronting Julian as the young man turned sharply towards him.

"What do you mean?" said Julian. "Are there any in the market?"

"Well, yes," said Loring quietly. "The fact is, there's a certain shooting in Scotland which I have coveted for years. It's for sale now, and on uncommonly reasonable terms. Of course, it's appalling extravagance on my part, for the shares are going up every day. But I am going to sell a thousand pounds' worth of Welcomes to-day and buy that moor."

"It is extravagance!" said Julian, and there was an eager light in his blue eyes.

"Like to have the shares?" said Loring imperturbably.

Julian hesitated.

"I should like them, of course," he said, rather breathlessly. "So would lots of other fellows. But, you see, my thousands, what there were of them, are all locked up in the Welcome already."

"You wouldn't think it worth while to borrow, I suppose?" enquired Loring carelessly.

"There's a little difficulty known as security."

"For some fellows, of course," was the answer. "But not for you. You've got money coming to you."

Julian coloured a dull red, and looked down at the carpet, moving his foot to and fro uneasily.

The idea of raising money on a reversion for such a purpose was for the moment inexpressibly repugnant to him.

"The shares are going up every day," said Loring; "you ought to make a good thing of it; and you'll sell at the end of this week, I take it? However, of course, I don't want to press you. They'll go off fast enough."

Julian lifted his head suddenly, and drove his clenched hand deep down into his pocket.

"I'll do it," he said. "All right, Loring, I'll take them."

"To-day?" said Loring suavely.

"To-day!" returned Julian, almost fiercely.

He turned and left the room abruptly, without another word. And Loring, with the smile of the night before touching his lips once more, took up his paper again. Apparently he had forgotten the letter he had received from South Africa on the previous day, and the news it contained.

CHAPTER VII

IT was six o'clock on the following day, and in the sunset light of the July evening—a light with which the bustling, hurrying, unlovely crowd on which it fell seemed strangely out of harmony—the current of human life was setting strongly in every direction from the City. Along Cornhill, going against the stream, but driven, nevertheless, at a pace which was looked upon far from favourably by the police occupied in regulating the traffic, there came a hansom cab. In the cab, with one hand gripping the doors until the knuckles stood out white, was Julian Romayne. His hat was pulled slightly forward over his brow, as if with some half-conscious sense of the ghastliness of his face, some instinct to hide that ghastliness from casual eyes. His face was of a livid pallor. There were grey shadows about the mouth, which was set into hard lines of temporary and difficult self-control. His nostrils, not sensitive as a rule, quivered slightly as the pace of his horse slackened perforce now and again; he gave no other slightest sign of consciousness of his surroundings.

The cab turned out of Cornhill, and in another second pulled up suddenly. Almost before the cab had stopped, Julian flung open the doors and leapt out. He paid the man double his fare, dashed into the building before which they had stopped, and up the stairs to an office on the second floor. His hand was shaking like a leaf as he stretched it out to try the lock of the door. It yielded to his touch, and he flung it roughly open and passed rapidly in. The outer office had only one occupant, a rather feeble-looking little man, who was trying to improve the appearance of a shabby hat by a careful application of his coat-sleeve. He looked up with a start on Julian's entrance, and an expression of comprehending concern dawned on his face. He was the messenger of the Welcome Diamond Mining Company. Before he could speak, however, a hoarse, peremptory question broke from Julian:

"Mr. Ramsay's not gone?"

"Not yet, sir," was the answer, given with timid alacrity. "He's here later than usual to-night, you see, in consequence———"

But before the first words were fairly uttered, Julian had crossed the room, and as he reached the second door leading into the inner office, it opened quietly, and Ramsay stood on the threshold. He was looking as imperturbable and uninterested as usual, and his voice was dry indifference itself as he observed:

"I have been expecting you all day."

Without a word Julian strode past him into the manager's room, and then, as Ramsay shut the door calmly, he said, in a quick, unnatural tone, which also carried with it a curious suggestion that he had not even heard Ramsay's words:

"It's a mistake! It's a mistake! It must be!"

Ramsay's only answer was a slight shrug of the shoulders as his dull eyes rested, apparently with complete indifference, upon Julian's face; and the latter went on, rapidly and unevenly:

"I've only just heard. I've been out of town all day. I've come to hear—to see what can be done."

The last words were hardly audible, as though his mouth was so parched that he could hardly articulate. He lifted his hand as if involuntarily, and pushed back his hat, fixing a pair of fierce, burning eyes upon Ramsay.

"There's nothing to be done, of course," said Ramsay drily. "The thing's collapsed."

A harsh, wild laugh rang through the room, its faint echoes startling the little man in the outer office.

"Collapsed!" cried Julian. "Collapsed, by Heaven!"

He put out one hand gropingly, caught at a chair near him and dropped heavily into it, letting his face fall forward upon his folded arms as they rested upon its back.

Only half an hour had passed since he had gone to his rooms in the Temple after a picnic on the river, to find waiting for him there a telegram from Ramsay. And into that half-hour had been compressed such a desperate stand against despair as is little less terrible than despair itself. The telegram had told him that on the opening of the Stock Exchange that morning it had been spread abroad on unimpeachable authority that the Welcome Diamond Mine was under water. This evening, the inevitable sequel of such a fact, as he knew too well, shares in the Welcome Diamond Mining Company were so much waste-paper.

Ramsay stood for a moment looking at him, with a rather curious expression on his inexpressive face.

"It's a turn of the game," he said drily. "If you stand to win, you must stand to lose, too. You hadn't thought of that, I suppose?"

With a sudden tumultuous movement, as though his agony of mind was no longer to be endured in stillness, Julian sprang from his chair and began to walk up and down the room with hasty, uneven strides.

"Thought of it!" he cried. "What was there to make one think of it? It was a certainty yesterday, man; a certainty!"

A spasm passed across his face, and seemed to cut off his words, and Ramsay observed sententiously:

"It's a mistake to reckon anything as a certainty till you hold it in your hand."

Julian faced round suddenly and confronted him, his eyes blazing, every feature working.

"What the devil is the good of saying things like that?" he demanded. "Can't you understand that I have reckoned on it, as you call it? Can't you understand that it was all or nothing with me, and I am just done? Can't you understand——"

He broke off suddenly, and, turning away with a heavy groan, flung himself into a chair, and let his face fall forward on the table. For all that he was face to face with at that moment he could have found no words. The remorse, the sense of failure and helplessness, the despair which seemed to be tearing his heart to pieces, were one intolerable anguish.

Ramsay followed him with his eyes, and then crossed the room quietly, and stood beside his bowed figure, which was shaken now and again from head to foot.

"Is it so bad as this, boy?" he said quietly. Then, as there came no answer, he went on meditatively: "Ten thousand pounds! Ten thousand isn't so much to lose. Counters in the game, that's all."

He paused, and after a moment Julian lifted his face, haggard and drawn.

"It's the stake you must look to," he said. "My stake was heavy, Ramsay. Oh, you're right enough. Ten thousand pounds isn't much. I borrowed a thousand yesterday—raised it on a reversion—to get hold of some shares Loring wanted to sell. That wasn't much either, of course."

He had spoken in a dreary, monotonous voice, which was inexpressibly hopeless. And Ramsay's eyes were fixed keenly on him as their owner said drily:

"You bought a thousand pounds' worth of Loring's shares yesterday? Did you know that he was selling out all his interest in the Welcome?"

Julian turned with a quick, startled movement, and then paused.

"All his interest?" he repeated. "He wanted a thousand to pay for a Scotch moor, that was all."

"He sold every share he had yesterday," returned Ramsay. "Curious coincidence."

"You don't mean to tell me——"

The eyes of the two men met; and Julian sprang to his feet with a fierce imprecation.

"He knew it?" he cried; "he knew it, and kept it dark, that he might keep the market to himself? It isn't possible, Ramsay; it isn't possible!"

"Nothing is impossible," returned Ramsay quietly.

A savage, hissing breath came from between Julian's set teeth, and he seemed literally alive with passion. Without a word he stretched out his hand for his hat and turned to leave the room. Ramsay quietly intercepted his passage.

"Where are you going?" he said.

"I'm going to see Mr. Loring."

The slightest possible smile touched the elder man's lips, and he said:

"All right. I shall have something to say to Mr. Loring, too. But listen to me, first. Was it a desperate necessity to you to pull off this affair?"

Julian did not speak. His lips twitched for a moment, then settled into a thin line; and the look in his eyes was answer enough.

"Very good, then," said Ramsay. "Come and see me here to-morrow at six. I may be able to give you a hand."

With a gesture of uncomprehending assent, but with no word of answer, Julian turned away and left the room.

Three-quarters of an hour later he was coming rapidly down the staircase which led from Loring's chambers. His face was flushed and quivering, and every pulse was beating madly, like the pulses of a man who has just given unrestrained expression to furious passion. He turned on to the Embankment, and began to walk away in a headlong fashion, evidently neither knowing nor caring where he was going.

And as he walked the tumultuous life and glow of his face died slowly out, and settled into a haggard, sullen mask of dull despair. He had spoken his mind to Loring, and now there was nothing more for him to do.

CHAPTER VIII

"WE are all the slaves of man, my dear Lady Bracondale. You are kept in town because Parliament insists on keeping your husband; and I am kept in town because—oh, because the most capricious young man in London happens to be my son!"

An afternoon call in the first week of August is distinctly an anomaly, and seems to partake somewhat of the nature of a visit of condolence. Parliament was sitting late this year, and those hapless wives who considered it their duty to wait in town until their legislating husbands were released, visited one another, and were visited by the one or two acquaintances detained in London by other causes, in a manner which betrayed a combination of martyrdom and shamefacedness.

Lady Bracondale, who was nothing if not a personification of duty done, or in the act of doing, was being condoled with, or called upon, on this particular August afternoon, by two distinct sets of sympathising acquaintances; two sets, which, in spite of placid words and pretty speeches, seemed to be entirely incapable of amalgamation; Mrs. Romayne, and Mrs. Pomeroy and her daughter, who had arrived a few minutes later. And it was to Mrs. Pomeroy that Lady Bracondale—who had a peculiar gift for saying in a stately and condescending manner the things which quicker perceptions would have recognised as not being precisely the best things to be said under the circumstances—turned, as Mrs. Romayne stopped speaking.

"I suppose Mrs. Romayne looks upon you as the exception that proves her rule," she said. "For it is not a case of manly compulsion with you, I believe? I hope your sister goes on well?"

Mrs. Pomeroy, having neither husband nor son, was detained in town by the presence in her house of the sister whom she had visited earlier in the year, and who had spent the last month under the care of a London doctor. But her tone was as placid as ever as she replied:

"Thank you, I believe they consider her nearly recovered, for the time being. She hopes to go home this week. And then Maud and I will go and pay some country visits. We don't think of going abroad this year. I shouldn't feel easy to be out of England while my sister remains in this state."

"But that's not compulsion at all!" exclaimed Mrs. Romayne gaily. "You are acting entirely on your own impulse. Now, just consider my hard case. We were going to Pontresina; you know I'm very fond of Pontresina; it's such a dear, bright, amusing place. And we were to have started yesterday. Now, imagine my feelings when, two nights ago, that boy of mine came home, and said that, on the whole, he thought he'd rather not go abroad this year; he's taken with an enthusiasm for his profession, if you please, and he must needs stay somewhere quiet—so he says—and work at it. I must do him the justice to say that he was awfully apologetic, dear fellow!" Mrs. Romayne laughed her little affected, maternal laugh. "He was very anxious that I should go without him, and even offered to give up his own plan when he found how preposterous I thought that part of his idea."

There was not the faintest difference in Mrs. Romayne's voice by which it would have been possible to tell that her last statement was even less veracious than any other part of her speech, and that Julian's proposal to give up his plan was a figment of the moment only.

"And then of course I gave in," she continued. "Of course, he knew I should—the wretch! And we're to have a cottage on the river, and spend six weeks there."

She finished with a little grimace, and Lady Bracondale observed politely:

"I'm afraid you will find it rather dull."

"I shall find it very dull," returned Mrs. Romayne with ingenuous frankness. "I shall be bored to death. But, then, you all know that I am really a very ridiculous woman, and if my lord and master is content, there is nothing more to be said. He's kind enough to assure me that there are lots of nice people about! I don't know what kind of nice people one is likely to find about the river in August and September, but I take his word for it."

"I believe the Comptons have a house-boat somewhere," observed Miss Pomeroy.

It was her first contribution to the conversation, and it was made apparently rather because conventionality by this time demanded a remark of some sort from her, than from any interest in the subject. Before any reply could be made, the door opened, and Marston Loring was announced.

Mrs. Romayne had been looking rather sharp-featured, and there was a great restlessness in her eyes. It seemed to leap up and then settle suddenly into comparative repose as they rested on Marston Loring, and as he turned to shake hands with her she greeted him gaily. It was their first meeting since the night of the Academy soirée, but Loring's manner was absolutely unmoved. His greeting to her differed in nowise from his greeting to the other two ladies, and if that fact in itself involved a subtle change in his demeanour towards her, the change was observed by one pair of eyes only—a pair of demure brown eyes. Miss Pomeroy had been a good deal interested in Marston Loring's comings and goings during the fortnight she spent in Queen Anne Street.

"I thought you were gone," Mrs. Romayne said lightly. "What are you doing in town to-day, may one ask, when you were booked to start for Norway yesterday?"

"Business," he returned in a tone which addressed the whole company rather than any member of it individually. "I am investing in a Scotch moor, and I can't leave London till I have signed and sealed."

There was a delicate implication of wealth about the statement which seemed to give a curious fillip to the conversation; and an animated discussion ensued on Scotland, its charms and its disadvantages.

Mrs. Romayne held her part in the discussion with unfailing readiness, and as the subject exhausted itself she rose to take leave. She said good-bye in her usual charming manner to her hostess, and to Mrs. Pomeroy and her daughter, and then she turned to Loring.

"By-the-bye," she said carelessly, "I've a piece of property of yours in the carriage. Did you know you had lost something when you called the other day? No, I shan't tell you what it is, you very careless person! But I'll give it you if you like to come down for it."

She turned away; Loring followed her perforce; and there was an ugly smile on his face as he did so. At the foot of the stairs she paused; then with a quick glance towards an open door which led into a dining room, she went rapidly towards it, signing to him to follow her. Once within the room, she turned and faced him. She was smiling still, but the smile was stiff and mechanical, and her eyes, as she fixed them on his face, were desperately anxious. There was a curious ring of conscious helplessness and reliance on the man to whom she spoke, about her voice as she began to speak.

"I wanted to speak to you," she said. "I'm so glad to see you. I'm rather perplexed. Julian has taken it into his head to stop in town, or, rather, close to town. He won't go abroad; he won't visit. Can you tell me the reason? Will you try and find out the reason? May I rely on you? But of course I know I may."

There was a tone almost of relief in her voice, as if in the mere making of the confidence, in the sense of companionship and support it gave her, she found some sort of ease.

And Loring smiled again as he met her eyes.

"I'm sorry to have to dispel an illusion which is so flattering to me," he said, with the slightest possible accentuation of his usual quiet cynicism of manner. "But it's useless to assume that I can be of any further service to you."

He stopped, watching with keen, relentless eyes the effect of his words. A startled look came to the face turned towards him. The eyebrows were lifted and contracted with a quick movement of perplexity. Evidently she believed that she had not fully understood him, for she did not speak, and he went on:

"Your son and I have quarrelled. He has insulted me grossly. For the future we are strangers to one another. Consequently you will see that I shall be no longer able to keep him out of mischief."

There was an indescribable tone in his voice, ominous and vindictive. And as he spoke, Mrs. Romayne's face seemed to grow old, and her eyes dilated.

"It can be put right," she said, in a quick, uncertain voice. "He will apologise. You will forgive——"

Loring interrupted her, very coldly and incisively.

"He will not apologise!" he said. "And I should not accept any apology. I needn't suggest, of course, that, under the circumstances, our acquaintance, much as I regret this, had perhaps better cease."

They faced each other for another moment, and into Mrs. Romayne's eyes there crept a sick despair strangely incongruous with the surface appearance of the position. Then she seemed to recover herself as if with a tremendous effort of will. She drew herself up, bowed her head with grave dignity, and moved to leave the room. He held the door open for her with an absolutely expressionless countenance. She passed down the hall to where the servant was waiting at the door, went out, and got into her carriage alone.

Loring stood at the foot of the stairs watching her, and then turned with a cruel contentment in his eyes, and went upstairs again to the drawing-room.

The two elder ladies were sitting with their heads very close together, as he opened the drawing-room door, evidently deep in some question of domestic importance. And standing by a conservatory window at the other end of the room, a rather bored-looking figure in its solitary girlishness, was Maud Pomeroy. The occasion being, as has been said, something of an anomaly, conventions were not so strict as usual. Lady Bracondale just glanced up with a vague smile as Loring reappeared, and then became absorbed in conversation as he strolled across to Maud Pomeroy. She looked up at him with a faint smile.

"Has Mrs. Romayne gone?" she said.

He signified a careless assent, and then said:

"You are looking rather bored, do you know, Miss Pomeroy? Suppose we go and look at the flowers until we're wanted?"

She hesitated a moment, and then moved idly into the conservatory, looking back at Loring with a smile as he followed her.

"I was a little bored," she confessed. "It is very kind of you to come and amuse me."

For the next moment or two Loring could hardly be said to prove himself very amusing. He sauntered round the little conservatory at his companion's side, his eyes fixed keenly upon her impassive profile with something very calculating in their depths. Miss Pomeroy also was apparently absorbed in thought, and did not notice his silence.

"You are a great friend of the Romaynes, are you not?" she said at last, in her thin, even, very "proper" tones.

Loring glanced at her again.

"Well," he said, "that's not a question that it's particularly easy for me to answer, to-day. I have been on fairly intimate terms with them, as you know. But do you know what that kind of thing sometimes leads to?"

Miss Pomeroy shook her head.

"Well, there is such a thing as knowing people too well," said Loring deliberately. "And then you find out little traits that don't do. To tell you the truth, Romayne and I have quarrelled."

"I'm glad of that," said Miss Pomeroy softly.

He looked at her quickly, but he was not quick enough to catch the spiteful gleam in her eyes.

"Would it be inquisitive to enquire why?" he said.

"I don't think Mr. Romayne is a nice young man," was the answer. "I would rather people I like———" She broke off in pretty confusion. "I would rather you weren't a friend of his, Mr. Loring. I think there's a great deal about him that nobody knows."

"Indeed!" said Loring, interrogatively and quietly.

"You see," she said, with charming seriousness, "I think a girl can often feel whether a man is nice or nasty quicker than another man can. Mr. Loring, has Mr. Romayne ever said anything to you—Oh, please don't think it's very odd of me to say such things to you! Has he ever said anything that made you think he might be married?"

There was a hardly perceptible pause—a hardly perceptible flash of comprehension on Loring's face, and the vindictive satisfaction in his eyes deepened.

"What makes you ask me that?" he said, in a tone which seemed to fence gravely with the suggestion rather than to repudiate it.

Miss Pomeroy responded with growing conviction.

"Because I'm quite sure that he is married. And, of course, as he doesn't own it, there must be something—something not nice about it. And it does seem to me so wrong that people should like him so much when he isn't a bit what they think he is."

The man's eyes and the girl's eyes met at that moment for the first time. The girl's were perfectly clear, mild, and expressionless, and into the man's there stole a cynical tinge of admiration.

"By Jove," he said to himself, "she is clever!"

At that instant Mrs. Pomeroy's voice was heard from the drawing-room calling placidly for her daughter. And Miss Pomeroy moved forward with graceful promptitude into the drawing-room.

"We shall meet in Scotland by-and-by, I believe," said Loring pleasantly, as he shook hands with Miss Pomeroy. "You were to be at the Stewarts', I believe, in the last week of September, and so am I. I shall look forward to it. Good-bye, Miss Pomeroy."

"Good-bye, Mr. Loring."

A few minutes later Loring also took leave of Lady Bracondale and went away. The satisfaction was stronger than ever in his eyes. Maud Pomeroy's words had somehow or other carried instantaneous conviction to his mind, and in the fact he believed them to contain he saw certain social ruin for Julian Romayne.

"He's done for himself all round," he said to himself as he let himself into his rooms half an hour later. "That nice little house in Chelsea will be to let next season."

At that same moment, in the manager's room at the offices of the Welcome Diamond Mining Company, Julian Romayne was standing by the table, looking down at Ramsay as the latter sat leaning back in his chair, indifferent enough in attitude, but with a hard intensity of expression in his dull eyes.

Julian had evidently just risen, pushing back his chair, the back of which he was gripping almost convulsively. His face was ashen, his eyes were dilated with an expression of desperate, intolerable temptation.

"I'll do it," he was saying in a harsh, unnatural voice. "I'll do it, Ramsay. Shake hands on it."

CHAPTER IX

THE cottage which Mrs. Romayne had taken for August and September, on Julian's refusal to go abroad, was situated a few miles above Henley. It was a very charming little house, to which the term "cottage" was applicable only in mock humility; and it was very charmingly situated. It had a delightful garden, not large, but full of "roses, and sunflowers, and all sorts of things," as Mrs. Romayne explained to Julian after her visit of inspection. Its lawns sloped down to the river, and altogether, on the same authority, it was a wonderful chance to get hold of it.

The statement which Mrs. Romayne had made to Lady Bracondale on Julian's authority, that there were "nice people about," had originated, as a matter of fact, not with Julian, but with his mother herself. It was quite true, nevertheless; but apparently Julian's sudden desire for quiet had proved infectious. The acquaintance between herself and her present neighbours being of the slightest, Mrs. Romayne made no such attempt as might have been expected of her to develope that acquaintance.

She seemed to be strangely without impetus in herself towards action of any kind. She was "resting," some people might have said; she was pausing, certainly. But whether, as the days went on, her life did not signify rather temporary and enforced quiescence, than the peaceful and pleasant suspension of labour, might have been an open question.

It was a hot, bright August; day after day the sun shone steadily down, as Julian departed for town after an early breakfast, at which his mother never failed to appear. Day after day it shone through all the long, little-broken hours upon the quiet house and garden, about which the one woman's figure moved in almost total solitude, until, with the evening, Julian returned again. Evening after evening the mother and son spent alone, but by no means always together. After their dinner, during which conversation seldom flagged between them, any more than it would have flagged between two friendly and well-bred acquaintances, Mrs. Romayne would sit in the drawing-room with a bit of fashionable fancy-work in her hand, into which she only occasionally put a stitch; and sometimes Julian would spend half an hour with her there, reading the newspaper and carrying on the talk of dinner; or sometimes he would stroll out into the garden at once, and come in only just before bed-time.

Mrs. Romayne never followed him and never questioned him. Perhaps it was the curiously still life she led which brought so strange and still an expression to her face; a stillness which suggested a slow, wearing waiting, and a mingled concentration, watchfulness, and patience.

It was an evening in the second week of September, and she was walking up and down the lawn in the fading sunset light. She was moving with slow, regular steps, with the monotonous motion of a woman to whom the even movement brought some sort of relief or soothing. There was an indescribable touch of desolateness about her lonely figure as she moved up and down before the empty house.

A servant came out to her by-and-by with some newly-arrived letters. She took them, and then, her monotonous motion being perforce suspended, a sense of physical fatigue seemed to assert itself, and she sat down on a low basket-chair.

A sigh came from her as she did so, one of those sighs which in their unconsciousness are so suggestive of habitual suffering. She paused a moment, looking away into space with absent eyes. Then she seemed to rouse herself, and took up one of the letters as if forcing herself to seek relief from the current of her monotonous thoughts. She had opened the envelope and read the letter half through in a mechanical, uninterested way, when its contents seemed suddenly to arrest her attention. A change came to her expression, a change which in its slight quickening and revival showed how dulled, almost numbed, it had been before.

She turned once more to the beginning of the letter and read it again.

"G<small>LENFYLE</small>, R<small>OSS-SHIRE</small>.

"D<small>EAR</small> M<small>RS</small>. R<small>OMAYNE</small>,

"I am so sorry to have to ask you to postpone the visit which you had promised us for the end of this month. I find that by some stupid mistake my husband and I have given separate invitations for the same date. As there is, unfortunately, no doubt that his invitation was given first, there falls upon me the very disagreeable task of explaining the situation to you and your son, and begging you to forgive me.

"Yours truly,

"M<small>ARION</small> S<small>TEWART</small>."

Mrs. Romayne leant back in her chair, not indolently, but with an intent consideration in every line of her figure; and letting the hand that held the letter fall on her knee, she sat gazing at the written words with sharp, angrily sparkling eyes, which looked as though they were bent on piercing through the words themselves to the meaning which she believed they hid. She was evidently surprised and annoyed; as evidently she gave not an instant's credence to the reason alleged for the postponement of the visit in question; and the slight involved in this postponement, indefinite, as she noticed with an unpleasant little smile, seemed to stimulate her.

Her face had grown even vindictive, when her eyes fell on the postmark of the second letter lying on her knee. It was that of the same little Scotch town, the name of which was stamped upon the already opened envelope. She took it up eagerly, and as she saw the handwriting, she paused for an instant, and a flash of intense consideration passed across her face. Then she tore it hastily open. It was from Mrs. Pomeroy, and it conveyed in three long-winded and incoherent sheets a piece of news which the writer was sure would delight Mrs. Romayne.

"Dear Maud," the letter said, was just engaged to "that charming Mr. Loring." Mrs. Pomeroy's mind seemed to be in a state of somewhat considerable confusion between a theoretical and conventional sense that it was very sad for her to lose her daughter, and a certain practical and actual sense, which by no means harmonised with the theoretical one, and all unconsciously threw a good deal of light on the relations between the mother and daughter, as they actually existed. The coherence of the letter was further disturbed by sundry sentences, which dovetailed so oddly into the general fabric that they had somewhat the appearance of being inserted to order; sentences which conveyed various repetitions of "dear Maud's" assurance of Mrs. Romayne's congratulations; and various repetitions of the statement that Mr. Loring's financial position had recently improved amazingly, and that he was sure of a seat in Parliament at the forthcoming general election.

"He has been staying with the Stewarts during the whole of our visit to them," the letter ended. "Dear Lady Marion has been so kind about it, and taken such an interest."

"Ah!"

The exclamation, uttered, evidently involuntarily, just above her breath, came from Mrs. Romayne's lips sharply and bitterly. She had read the letter through with certain quick movements of her eyebrows, and mocking smiles coming and going about her thin lips, and they smiled again as she folded the letter deliberately and put it back into its envelope. She was looking thoroughly roused now, and there was a confidence in her alert, determined expression. It was the kindling up of martial spirit at a challenging trumpet-call from a well-known battlefield.

If Marston Loring and his future wife were indeed arranging their forces for the undermining of Mrs. Romayne's social position—and Miss Pomeroy and Loring between them could have pieced out a very sufficient explanation of Lady Marion Stewart's note—the campaign, judging from appearances at that moment, was likely to be far from a tame one.

Mrs. Romayne was still sitting with the letters in her hand, tapping one foot with impatient vigour upon the grass, and there was the same eager intentness in her eyes, when from the house behind her the sound of a dinner-bell rang out. She started violently, and in the start something seemed to fall between her and the subject on which her thoughts had been busy. A curious shade of that new stillness replaced the energy on her face. It was the dressing-bell, and she rose mechanically; and as she turned towards the house her eyes fell upon the figure of Julian. He had evidently been standing on the verandah, and as she rose he had turned, and was disappearing into the house. Another shade of stillness fell upon her face, as though the letters she had received, and the feelings they had stirred, had receded into the distance.

It often happened that the mother and son did not meet, on Julian's return home in the evening, until dinner-time, and it happened so this evening. The dinner-bell was ringing when Julian came downstairs with a quick word or two of apology, and followed his mother into the dining-room.

Julian looked as though his month's hard work had by no means agreed with him. His face was even painfully thin and worn, and there was an expression of hard concentration about it which seemed to age it strangely. His eyes were rather sunken. It was a curious feature of a change in him less easily defined, that his likeness to his mother had faded considerably. All the character of his face now seemed to originate about his mouth; that mouth of which Mrs. Romayne had been wont to say with affected gaiety that it was like nobody in particular; that mouth which had been a somewhat weak and undecided feature. There was nothing undecided about it now, and Mrs. Romayne never looked at it without a deepening of that stillness on her face. It was set into heavy, resolute lines.

No one, indeed, judging from the bare outline of Julian's daily life during that hot August, could have wondered at the signs of physical wear and tear that he exhibited. Ten o'clock, on every one of those sultry days, found him at work, not indeed in the Temple, but in an office in the City; and it was from the same office that he would issue forth at about five o'clock to catch the train for Henley, sometimes with sullen determination, sometimes with a pale, fierce excitement on his face.

The affairs of the Welcome Diamond Mining Company had readjusted themselves, after the blow which had threatened the company's very existence, as hardly the most sanguine could have hoped. Ten days after the announcement of the presence of water in the mine, some of the newspapers published another telegram which had been received by the directors. The passage of the water, by which the existing mine was rendered practically useless, had revealed hitherto unsuspected possibilities, and there appeared to be little doubt that the first mine had been, as it were, only a pledge of still richer strata yet to be worked. One telegram followed another, confirming the report in greater detail. Prospectuses were issued, setting forth a proposal to utilise the opportunity thus opened, and debentures were issued for the providing of the necessary funds. These debentures were taken up somewhat slowly at first, but on the arrival in England of specimens of diamonds from the new lead, together with a circumstantial report, they were taken up with a rush. Works were understood to be already on foot, and dividends were looked for at an early date. The new managing director of the company was Julian Romayne.

There was a kind of dry excitement about him to-night behind the deliberate assumption of conversational interest which was his never-changing manner with his mother now, and his hand shook a little as he poured himself out more wine than usual.

He did not rejoin his mother in the drawing-room, saying something as she left him about having letters to write; and two hours afterwards he was walking up and down the lawn in the moonlight with a cigar.

There was a fierce restlessness in his step, and there was a fierce restlessness in his face, too. He had been walking there for half an hour when a shadow passed across the blind of the drawing-room window—the night was very hot and the window was wide open—and the blind was drawn up. Mrs. Romayne's figure stood there outlined by the lamplight within. The drawing-room window was shadowed from the moonlight by an angle of the house.

"Good night, Julian!" she called.

Julian stopped in his walk mechanically.

"Good night, mother!" he answered. The figure in the window seemed to hesitate for a moment; then Mrs. Romayne moved and drew down the blind, the lights in the room behind went out one by one, and Julian resumed his walk in the moonlight as mechanically as he had stopped it.

It was his custom to go, every morning, first to his room in the Temple in case any letters might be waiting for him there; and on the following morning, a slight accident on the line having considerably delayed his train, he paused a moment before giving his order to the cabman. He was very late, and there was a feverish impatience in every line of his face. He had almost decided that any private letters might wait until the next day, when, with a sudden, unaccountable reaction, he sprang into the cab and told the man to drive to the Temple.

He had apparently repented of the resolution by the time the cab stopped, for he sprang out with a muttered imprecation on the delay. There was only one letter waiting for him, and he caught it up fiercely. Then the handwriting in which it was directed caught his eye.

All the tumultuous heat and impatience of his face died out suddenly and utterly. He stood for a moment staring down at the letter, white to the very lips. Then he seemed absolutely and physically to set his teeth, and in the intense hardness of determination which set its mark on every muscle of his face, his whole expression would have seemed to deteriorate, markedly and terribly, but for the desperation in his eyes which was little short of agony.

He moved abruptly, crossed the room, unlocked a drawer in his writing-table, and thrust the letter in with quick, deliberate movements, unopened. He locked the drawer again sharply, and turned and went hastily out of the room.

The letter was from Clemence; it was the first sign of her existence which he had received since their parting on that June evening nearly three months ago.

He was looking only older, harder, and more recklessly resolute when about a quarter of an hour later he entered the office of the Welcome Diamond Mining Company. The feeble-looking little messenger was in solitary possession, and he looked up rather uneasily as Julian wished him a brief good morning and crossed to the door of the manager's room.

"Mr. Ramsay's just gone out, Mr. Romayne," he said. "I was to say he would be in again directly."

Julian made a curt gesture of assent and went on into the private room. There was plenty of work waiting for him, it appeared, and he was still applying himself to it with dogged concentration, when, nearly an hour later, the door opened and Ramsay appeared.

"There you are!" he said indifferently. "I thought you weren't going to turn up this morning."

Julian had just glanced up from the letter he was writing to acknowledge the other man's entrance, and he went on writing as he explained briefly that his train had been delayed.

"No particular reason for wanting me, I suppose?" he said in a brief, businesslike way, as he laid down his pen.

Ramsay sat down deliberately, and put his hand into the breast-pocket of his coat.

"Well, yes," he said. "There's a matter here which rather calls for the attention of the managing director."

He held out a letter as he spoke, and Julian took it and read it quickly. Then he laid it down on the table before him, and looked up slowly at Ramsay. His face was rather pale.

"A general meeting of shareholders!" he said. "Demanded!"

There was a moment's pause, while he looked steadily into Ramsay's immoveable face, and then he added in the same rather difficult tone:

"Did you expect this, Ramsay?"

"I never expect," returned Ramsay drily. "Such a thing was on the cards, of course."

Julian's face grew dark and calculating.

"Well," he said harshly, after another moment's pause, "it must be arranged for, of course. What do you propose?"

Ramsay answered the question by another.

"Do you happen to know anything," he said, "of a man named Compton—Howard Compton?"

Julian's brows contracted as if with an involuntary effort to detect the relevancy of the question as he answered tersely:

"Yes. He and I belong to the same club."

"You didn't know, I suppose, that some shares in the Welcome have drifted into his hands?"

Julian shook his head with a quick frown of vexation.

"Ah!" observed Ramsay; "they have, though. And it has come to my knowledge that various enquiries have been made into the state of the Welcome Diamond Mine; made on the spot, and made in secret. And I've traced these enquiries to this Mr. Howard Compton."

A dreadful grey pallor had begun to spread itself over Julian's face, and the muscles seemed to have grown rigid with the intense force with which he held them to their expression of dogged determination. He did not speak, and Ramsay went on in the same dry, indifferent way:

"He is either a very clever hand, or very cleverly advised. The one point we score, at present, is that he has not done as he intended to do, and taken us by surprise."

"Do you mean to say——"

The words seemed to come from between Julian's dry, white lips almost without consciousness on his part. His eyes were fixed upon Ramsay with a hard, unseeing kind of stare, his voice was hoarse, uneven, and hardly audible, and it died away, leaving the sentence unfinished.

"The meaning is obvious, of course," returned Ramsay. "An affair of this kind is a ticklish thing to pull off, and a hitch of this kind is always possible, though I never came across an affair in which it seemed less probable. I don't know yet exactly how much our friend knows. The meeting won't be a particularly placid affair, of course, and you're likely to have a warm time of it. But, of course, there's a chance that he mayn't know quite enough, and we may be able to pull it through, yet."

"And if not?"

Something seemed to rattle in Julian's throat as he spoke the words, and they came out thick and husky.

"If not?" repeated Ramsay. "Well, if not, I think I wouldn't go to that meeting if I were you."

There was a moment's dead silence, broken only by Julian's heavy, laboured breathing. The two men sat there face to face, and their eyes met with a terrible significance of what was better unexpressed in words. Then Ramsay's dull eyes took a deliberate survey of Julian's face. It was drawn and livid, and the elder man rose and took from the cupboard some brandy. He poured it into a glass with a slightly contemptuous smile, and put it into Julian's hand.

"You're the very devil to work," he said drily. "And for all I know you may be first-rate as a winner; but I can't say you're a good loser. And it's a useful lesson to learn in this business."

Julian drank the brandy and rose mechanically. The strong stimulant hardly seemed to touch the blanched horror of his face.

"What do you propose to do?" he said in a stiff, toneless voice.

"Personally, nothing," returned Ramsay, "until I know more. Business will go on as usual. You'll call the meeting, of course. I'll tell Harrison to get the forms ready for you to sign. They must be sent out to-morrow. Going?"

"Yes," said Julian heavily. "There's nothing more I need do to-day."

He took his hat and went slowly out of the office, looking straight before him like a man walking in his sleep. Ramsay looked after him, and stood for a minute rubbing his chin thoughtfully.

"Not quite what I thought he was," he said to himself; "though he has served this purpose well enough. Pity he hasn't a little more of his father in him. Got all the makings of the right sort, but he can't stay."

CHAPTER X

THE early sunlight of a lovely September morning was streaming into the room through every crack and chink in the blinds and curtains, making the light from the still burning lamp look yellow, dim, and unnatural. It was Julian's sitting-room in the house in Chelsea, and the light, falling here and there, touched into distinctness many of those little luxurious details on which the evening light had fallen on that winter day eighteen months before, when Mrs. Romayne had stood upon the threshold and looked round upon her completed arrangements, waiting then for the use which was to give them life. On a chair by the writing-table, his head dropped sideways on his arm as it rested on the table, sat Julian Romayne asleep.

He was asleep, but he was not at rest. His face was grey and drawn; it twitched painfully, and his hand was fiercely clenched. Gradually an expression of terror and despair gathered on his features, until they were almost convulsed, and with a strangled, gasping cry he woke and started to his feet, trembling in every limb, and with great drops standing on his forehead. He stood clutching at a chair for support, while the first poignant impression of his dream subsided, and then he moved as though impelled by some reactionary impulse to collect himself. He glanced at the clock and saw that the hands pointed to a quarter past six. He was vaguely conscious of having heard it strike six, so that he could have slept for a few moments only. His lips twitched slightly at the thought of what those few moments had held for him. Then he realised that he was cold, that all his limbs were stiff and aching, and he dragged himself slowly across the room, drew the curtains and the blinds, and stood there in the sunshine.

It was the first movement of physical consciousness which he had felt since he left the office of the Welcome Diamond Mining Company on the morning of the previous day.

How that day had passed he did not know. Here and there in the blackness a picture of himself stood out with uncertain distinctness. He knew that he had telegraphed to his mother to the effect that he might not return to Henley for some time. He remembered writing the words though he could recall no mental process by which the elaborate excuse he had made had occurred to him. He knew that somewhere dinner had been placed before him, though where, and whether he had eaten, he knew not at all. For the rest, an impression of ceaseless walking, of interminable streets giving place imperceptibly to the four walls of his own room, made up the only actual background in his memory to the intense mental consciousness which had usurped for the time being the tangibility of material things.

The favourable turn in the affairs of the Welcome Diamond Mining Company had been founded on a deliberate system of forgery and fraud, planned by Ramsay, subscribed to and participated in by Julian. The telegram as to the new lead had been concocted in the office in the City; the diamonds exhibited as earnest of the future yield of the mine had been bought for that purpose; and not one penny of the money paid in debentures had ever been intended for application to the working of the ruined mine. If these facts should come to light—and hostile enquiries once instituted on the spot, only one of those incredibly lucky chances to which gamblers and swindlers alike owe so much could avert such a catastrophe—the consequences were obvious. Public exposure, public ignominy and execration, wholesale and irremediable loss of position, were absolutely inevitable. And as inevitable if he remained in England, the dark gulf in which his life must be swallowed up and closed—as far as everything which constituted life for him was concerned—whether he fled from it or whether it clutched him, was the legitimate reward of his doings; penal servitude.

He could not realise it. He could not face it. He had beaten it back, he had thrust it down again and again during that long day and night, and again and again the horror had swept over him, gaining always in certainty and reality. Struggle against it as he might and did, clutching at his consciousness, shaking and rending it with a force not to be resisted, and growing ever stronger and stronger, there dawned a dazed, bewildered conviction that the end he saw before him was indeed the inevitable end; that in that black gulf, and no other, all his efforts and fierce strivings were to find their consummation.

He had digged it with his own hands; he had followed on towards it in a very desperation of defiance and recklessness, goaded by a grinding sense of failure and frustration to a wild daring which had looked like courage and resolution. But the spirit which had stimulated him was not in himself. All unconscious of it as he was, he had been drunk with the thought of what lay beyond that gulf; drunk with a desperate, unreasoning anticipation of triumph. The hideous possibility of failure confronted him now practically for the first time, and before it all his fictitious stamina shrivelled away, as in its very nature it was bound to do. A vague, confounded comprehension of the consequences which he had brought upon himself rose upon him, walling him in on every side; and about those consequences, as connected with himself, there was all the ghastly incongruity and unreality of a hideous nightmare. He had never understood the realities of life. He had crushed down their impulses in his heart. He had called superficialities essentials; selfish ignorance, practical sense; and he had worked and fought in a false atmosphere, and for a false aim.

And now, instead of that fictitious triumph which he had looked to grasp, he found himself face to face with facts so sordid and so relentless that he could hardly recognise them as facts at all. His world was tottering into ruins all about him; the clash and crisis of imminent downfall and disgrace was stunning him and shaking him through and through; and in the wild tumult and confusion all the limitations of his nature seemed to break up, as it were, into one blind chaos of protest and repudiation, dominated only by despair. Nothing fixed or steadfast held its place. The very passions by which he had been driven on had been borne down and numbed. The thought of Clemence had become merely a vague element in the confusion. Of his mother he did not think at all. Even that dark factor in his being—the perversion of his instincts as to truth and falsehood, honesty and dishonesty—which had asserted its grim presence with the very awakening of his character; which had dictated the first steps along the path of which he stood now at the end; was swept into solution, now, with every other element in his character. It had held its place, hitherto, side by side with the other motive powers by which his life had been regulated; dictating the lines on which those powers should work, strengthening and developing with the demands they put upon it. But it had remained the servant of a stronger passion, and as far as any power of support or guidance was concerned it had gone down in the flood. He had no perception, truly, of the moral aspect of his position, no sense of guilt or of remorse. He only knew that he was beaten, that it was all over with him.

He stood there at the window staring out into the sunshine, seeing nothing, conscious of nothing but the gulf before him; as utterly and absolutely isolated in his misery as though he had been the only creature living in the world. The desperate struggle with facts was sinking into a hopeless confused acceptance of them; into a dazed, bewildered contemplation of details which seemed to rise slowly into distinctness out of the fog which hung about them; to rise and fade again without volition on his part. Details connected with the future came first, and he looked at them and understood them with stunned composure as though they stood outside him all together. Then he found himself wondering heavily as to the time that must pass before the certainty that was in himself became literal knowledge. There was no sense of any possible chance of salvation in his mind.

By-and-by he became heavily and confusedly aware that another day had begun; another day through which he must carry his horrible, bewildering burden—no longer in the semi-unconsciousness of yesterday, but alive now in every fibre to its intolerable pressure.

He went out into the sunshine by-and-by, out into the streets he knew so well; and as he walked along there came upon him a ghastly sense of being but a shadow among shadows. The life about him seemed to have receded to an incalculable distance, to have lost all substance. He himself, as he appeared to other people, had no existence; and his real self had no existence for any one but himself. He was face to face with black, implacable reality, and before its presence all the superficialities and conventionalities which had usurped its place vanished like the shades they were.

He walked, always with that chill sense of isolation on him, from Chelsea to the City; in motion, in continual motion only, was his misery endurable. Ramsay was not at the office when he arrived, and a message from him, left with the secretary, informed Julian that he would not be there that day. His absence affected Julian not at all. There was no suspense in his mental attitude to make him crave for even a blow to end it. To his battered consciousness delay before the final agony had something of the appearance of rest or respite. He did the work he had come to do with a numbed comprehension of its import, and then as he passed out again into those horribly unreal streets there came upon him a desperate longing for human companionship; a desperate longing to break through his solitude and touch another human creature. He would go to the club, he thought dully. He must speak to some one; he must get some assurance of his own identity, or its unfamiliarity would drive him mad.

There were two or three men only who were known to him in the room when he arrived, and even as they greeted him they seemed to elude him; to retreat and to lose all tangibility beyond the yawning gulf which lay between himself and them. He tried to talk, he tried desperately to bridge the gulf. In vain. He turned away and went out into the streets again, alone with the one terrible reality which the world seemed to contain.

The failure broke him down. An unendurable horror of himself and of the world; a very terror of his misery; rolled down upon him and overwhelmed him. It was one of those realisations of the impotency of humanity before the strokes of the infinitely greater than humanity which seize upon a man sometimes when all the wrappings of life and custom are stripped from him, and he finds himself in primeval defencelessness. He could only fight wildly with it. Those instincts and affinities through which such moments work out strength and comprehension were utterly submerged in him, now; the experience could be for him nothing but a blind horror, giving place at last to the old stunned, hopeless confusion and despair. And when at last he dragged himself upstairs to his room in the Temple late at night he was utterly exhausted, mentally and physically. He dropped into a chair and sank into a heavy sleep.

Ten days followed; ten long days giving place to heavy nights; ten nights passing into monotonous days. By degrees Julian fell into a species of dull routine, in which he ate and drank, and even slept; passed to and fro along the London streets; stunned almost to stupefaction. He went each day to the office and sat there all day long doing little; sitting, for the most part, staring into space or walking up and down with heavy, regular steps. He was rarely disturbed. Ramsay appeared but seldom; his visits were brief, and he was uncommunicative.

At last there came a morning when he reached the office to find upon his desk a letter in Ramsay's familiar handwriting.

Julian sat down before it and looked at it for a moment, his face twitching slightly. Then he broke the seal.

"Dear Romayne," he read,—

"Your friend, Compton, holds the whole affair in his hand. Marston Loring gave him the tip. You will do as you think best about meeting the shareholders. I shall not be present myself, as I am leaving England, for the present, to-night.

"Yours,

"Alfred Ramsay."

The letter bore date of the previous day.

CHAPTER XI

A WHITE face, drawn and set into a look which pitifully travestied the calmness of despair; bloodshot eyes with something in them of the incomprehending agony of a hunted animal; quivering lips which would not take the rigid line at which they aimed, and from which seemed to radiate an indescribable suggestion of youthfulness, which made the bewildered desperation of the face infinitely piteous. Two hours had passed, and Julian was seated at his writing-table in his room at the Temple. He held a pen in his hand, and before him lay a sheet of paper bearing three words only, "My dear Clemence." On the table behind him lay a roughly packed travelling-bag and a "Bradshaw."

Flight, instant flight, was the one course that had occurred to him. Such a necessity had been present to him from the first, and in the almost insane terror which had mastered him on finding himself deserted by Ramsay, thoughts which had lain dormant in his mind during the last ten days had taken shape almost without volition on his part, and he had made his plans with wild haste. He knew nothing, he thought of nothing but that he must go at once, that at any moment he might find himself stopped, at any moment it might be too late!

No thought of that last refuge of the detected criminal, suicide, presented itself to him. The realities of life were as yet strange to him; wrenched from his moorings, tossed away to drift on the pitiless sea, he could not realise what was the depth of that sea, how futile must be his struggles to keep himself afloat. The reality of death had never touched his superficial nature.

He made his preparations with the promptitude of desperation, and as each detail was despatched, one deed that must be done began to prick into his consciousness. Some word must be sent to Clemence. With this necessity he found himself at last confronted with no further possibility of postponement.

But no words would come to him. Little as he understood it, all the bewildered misery of his heart was what he wanted to convey to her; all the incoherent horror which was tossing him to and fro. What words were possible where there was no reason, only blind, agonised feeling? There was one aspect of his shipwreck now in which it appeared only as the end and consummation of his ten weeks of silence towards Clemence; those ten weeks in which he saw, now, only cruelty and futility where he had seen before wisdom and necessity. His failure, his ruin, had a side on which they touched him only in his connection with her; it became the failure to keep the promise he had made her when he saw her last; the ruin of his vision of a life with her. He sat there, staring stupidly at the paper, and gradually all thoughts slipped away from him but the thought of Clemence herself. A hunger, such as his selfish young heart had never known, rose in him for her presence, her pity. His misery turned to her, stretching forth empty, despairing hands, until the sick longing dominated his whole consciousness.

Then out of the aching yearning there came to him suddenly a recollection of the letter he had received ten days before; the letter which he had thrust into a drawer, in his blind, foolhardy determination, unopened. The end on which he had set himself to wait had vanished for ever. Everything by which he had held was overturned and submerged. But the letter was there still. The letter had come from Clemence.

He unlocked with trembling eagerness the drawer in which he had placed it, drew out the envelope and tore it open. That it could bring no comfort to him, that there could, indeed, be only aggravation of his wretchedness in it, was as nothing to him. It was to touch Clemence that he wanted; Clemence, and Clemence only was the cry of his whole being. The letter was very short, a few lines only. He ran his eyes over it with hungry avidity, and then they seemed to stop suddenly, and all the quivering life seemed to freeze on his features. A moment passed and a great, dry sob broke from him; he dashed his head down upon the table with a bitter boyish cry:

"Clemmie! Clemmie!"

Simple, beautiful with that wonderful new tenderness which comes to a woman with the consummation of her womanhood, pathetic in their gentleness beyond all words, the few brief lines brought him from Clemence the most sacred tidings that can pass between husband and wife, tidings of the birth of their child.

"Clemmie!"

The word broke from him again, a pitiful, despairing sob, and then he lay there, long, dry sobs shaking him from head to foot as that bitterest of all waves, the unavailing realisation of what might have been contrasted with what is, swept over him and overwhelmed him. The reality, touched into life by her letter as though Clemence's voice had spoken to him, which he had thrown away; the reality on which, in doing so, he had hurled himself; stood out before him in pitiless distinctness; and in his ignorance and blindness, in his utter want of comprehension of the moral aspect of his acts and the stern justice of the retribution he was meeting, there was no light or cohesion for him anywhere in the world, and darkness and chaos had closed about him.

Nearly an hour passed before he moved, and lifted a white, haggard face, marred with the agony of impotent regret. He looked about him vaguely, pushing his hair back heavily from his forehead, and as his eye fell upon the travelling-bag that instinctive sense of the necessity upon him, which had stirred him with no consciousness on his part, deepened into a mechanically active impulse. He must go. He paused a moment, and then he drew out a fresh sheet of paper.

"Falconer!" he muttered. "Falconer will see to them. There's no one else!"

It was as though the fire through which he was passing had burnt away from him all recollection, even, of his mother. He had thought of her for long only as the source of all that was unpleasant in his life. Now in the sharpness of his pain a haze had spread itself over the past, and all thought of the means by which the present position had been brought about was obliterated.

He wrote for a few minutes, rapidly, desperately, in a handwriting which was hardly legible; then he thrust the letter into an envelope, which he directed to Dennis Falconer; and rose. His original intention of writing to Clemence had left him. It had become an impossibility. And side by side with his sense of his utter incapacity to find any words in which to speak to her, there had risen in him a heart-broken impulse to see her face once more and for the last time.

The sunshine of the day had given place to a drizzling rain when he turned into that quiet little street which had witnessed their last meeting. The dazed sense of the necessity for flight was strong upon him. Darkness had fallen; he had left his room for the last time; in another hour he would be in the Liverpool train, a fugitive from justice; and in the terror and confusion of the realisation of that one all-absorbing fact, the only other thought that lived in him was his blind desire for one sight of Clemence. He had come to the little street unreasoningly, weighing no probabilities as to whether or no she would be at work; not even understanding that there were probabilities to weigh; coming there simply because he had seen her there before and knew of no other chance of seeing her. He took up his position in a doorway by which she must pass, and waited. It seemed to him that he had been standing there, utterly alone, for hours, when the door, from which his haggard, sunken eyes had never stirred, opened.

As on that other occasion Clemence was the last to come out, but she came this time walking quickly and eagerly. For an instant as she passed beneath the lamp the light fell on her face, and as Julian's eyes rested on it for that instant, he clutched at the railing by which he stood. Then she came on in the shadow, still followed by those hungry eyes.

Perhaps she felt their gaze. Perhaps her own heart felt the pang that was rending his. In the very act of passing him she stopped suddenly and turned towards him, looking into the dimness in which he was shrouded. She stretched out her hands with a low, inarticulate cry.

He had her in his arms in an instant, straining her to him with a despairing passion which he had never known before, and she clung to him half frightened by his touch.

"Julian!" she whispered. Then as no word came from him, only his burning kisses pressed upon her upturned face, she went on softly: "Dear, weren't you going to speak to me?" Still he did not speak, and with a look and accent indescribably beautiful in their tender womanliness, she said: "You didn't think I would reproach you?"

"It's good-bye, Clemmie," he muttered hoarsely. "Good-bye! I—I'm going away for—for a little while."

He could as easily have killed her, at that moment, as have told her the truth.

"Going away!" she echoed, with a little catch in her breath. "Where, dear?"

"To—to America." He could not tell her all the truth, but there was no power in him to originate an unnecessary lie. He felt her arms tighten about him, and he answered the appeal hoarsely, hurrying out the words. "I—I'm leaving a letter about you, and——" his voice died away in his throat as he tried to speak of his child, and then he went on rapidly and unevenly: "It will be—all right. Clemence! Clemence! try to forgive me. Good-bye, dear, good-bye!"

He drew her hands from about his neck, kissing them wildly. Her hold tightened instinctively upon his fingers, and she was trembling very much.

"You're not going—now?" she whispered.

"Yes," he answered hoarsely. "Now!"

Then, as he saw the look which came over her face, the desperate necessity for reassuring her came upon him. He tried to smile.

"America is nothing nowadays, you know," he said in a harsh, unnatural tone. "It's no distance. I shall be—back directly. Say good-bye to me, won't you? I must go."

She let her face fall on his shoulder, pressing it closer and closer, as though she could never tear herself away.

"I'm frightened for you, dear," she said. "I'm frightened. Are you sure, sure, there is nothing—wrong?"

"Quite sure—of course."

"You will be back soon?"

"Quite soon."

There was a moment's quivering silence, and then Clemence slowly lifted her face. He took her in his arms again, and their lips met in one long agonised kiss. Neither spoke again. When he released her, Julian, with a face like death, turned and went away down the street, his head bent, his whole figure tense as though he were facing a blinding wind. Clemence stood for a moment still as a statue, her eyes wide, her face quite quiet. Then she too went away through the night.

CHAPTER XII

OVER the country about Henley, that same day, the sun was shining gloriously.

It was about five o'clock in the afternoon, and there was a clearness about the light, a distinctness about the shadows, which, taken in conjunction with the heavy bank of clouds into which the sun would presently sink, argued coming rain. For the present, however, nature was lovely to look at; and a garden-party which was going on in the large, old-fashioned garden of a large, old-fashioned country house, about a mile from the river, had the benefit of every advantage which atmosphere and surroundings could give.

It was a large party, and the scene was very bright and animated. On the larger of the two lawns, conspicuous among the well-dressed but by no means striking-looking women about her, stood Mrs. Romayne, talking to a local magnate.

She had arrived about half an hour before, and the politely concealed satisfaction and surprise with which she had been received had testified to the fact that her appearance at such a function was a phenomenon in the neighbourhood. Invitations had showered in on her during her residence at the "cottage," but it had gradually become an established fact that she was "going out very little." This was in truth the first party she had attended. It was fortunate that her hostess was not a particularly observant person. There had been something about Mrs. Romayne when she arrived which might have dashed that hostess's personal elation with a suspicion that her guest's appearance had been dictated by motives not wholly complimentary to the party; lines about the mouth which suggested the enforced endurance of a burden from which she was seeking temporary relief, however fictitious; a restlessness in the eyes which suggested an attempt at the eluding of the too insistent companionship of her own thoughts.

Her eyes were painfully bright, and there was a nervous tension about her manner as she stood there on the lawn, talking and laughing. But her companion of the moment—a worthy old gentleman, with not much acquaintance among women of the world—thought her simply the most astonishingly charming woman he had ever met; and seeking in his mind for lines on which to make himself agreeable to her, he recollected to have heard something about her son.

"You have a son here, I believe?" he said, with ponderous interest. "I should greatly like to make his acquaintance."

Mrs. Romayne laughed.

"I have a son," she said, "but he is not here, I'm sorry to say. He is hard at work just at present. Ah!" she broke off with an exclamation of surprise. "I see a friend of mine over there! I must go and speak to her." And with a bow and a smile to her admirer, she broke off the conversation which had, perhaps, seemed longer to one party than to the other, and moved across the lawn to where Hilda Compton was standing watching her with an uncertain but not particularly pleasant expression on her pretty face.

"Are you staying in the neighbourhood?" said Mrs. Romayne prettily, when they had shaken hands. She was apparently entirely oblivious of something cold and disagreeable in the younger woman's manner. "Is your husband here?"

Hilda Compton glanced at her with a certain tentative triumph in her eyes.

"No!" she said. "He's not here. I'm staying on a house-boat, but he is kept in town over some troublesome business!"

She paused, and then, as Mrs. Romayne made a rather patronising gesture of sympathy, that gleam of triumph strengthened into something distinctly malicious. Hilda Compton had never forgotten or forgiven that moment in the Norfolk garden twelve months ago. It had been no part of her policy to resent it when such resentment must necessarily have rebounded to her own disadvantage; she had accepted Mrs. Romayne's society friendliness during the past season with just such a manner as might sting but could not, in very self-respect, be impugned by the elder woman; a manner cleverly tinged with that deference which points the sense of superiority with which a certain type of girl recognises the fact that the present is to her, and not to the previous generation. But she had hoped always that the day might come when she would find herself in a position to take more active measures, and she felt, now, that even what she knew to be a slight breach of conjugal faith would be venial, if it would straighten what she would have called her "score" against Julian Romayne's mother.

"Yes, it's rather a bore!" she said. "City business, you know! Don't you think it's very foolish of men to speculate, Mrs. Romayne? Of course I haven't a quarter of your experience, but I think so. They always seem to get into trouble of some sort! But you know more than I do about this affair, no doubt, since Mr. Romayne is mixed up in it, and he's such a devoted son. Husbands don't tell one much, I find!"

Self-command is a wonderful thing, even when it originates in no higher motive than the instinct of a woman of the world for the retention of her society demeanour. Mrs. Romayne's lips were ashen and her fingers were clenched round the sunshade she held until her rings cut into them, but she faced Hilda Compton steadily, and with a mechanical smile, her eyes, a little dull and contracted, meeting the girl's pretty, unfeeling ones. Hilda Compton noticed the change of colour even behind the artificial tinting, and rejoiced at the slip of the tongue by which her foolish young husband had put such a weapon into her hand. If only she had succeeded in making Howard tell her more, instead of making him lose his temper! She reflected, however, that perhaps the truth was not so very bad after all, and hints might possibly sound worse than the actual facts.

"Do tell Mr. Romayne, from me, that I hope he hasn't done anything very shocking!" she said, with a laugh. "I wanted Howard to tell me just what it was, but he would not. Isn't it funny how men seem to lose their heads altogether when they get on to that silly Stock Exchange? The last men one would expect, too! Who would have thought of Mr. Romayne's getting into trouble of that kind?"

Somewhat to her disgust, Hilda Compton found as she proceeded that it was impossible to give such significance to her words as she would have wished. She realised that it would never do to allow herself to be brought to book, and consequently conventionality demanded that she should adopt a jesting tone, and trust to Mrs. Romayne's possessing some half knowledge which should give the words the barb she wished for them. She had a pleasant conviction, as Mrs. Romayne answered her, that she had done something, at least, towards wiping out that old score. The elder woman's words were preceded by a harsh little laugh, and there was something indistinct about their utterance.

"Just so. Who would have thought———"

Mrs. Romayne stopped abruptly, and a sharp, extraordinary spasm passed across her face, leaving it fixed and old.

The girl by her side could not flatter herself that the effect was produced by her words, for Mrs. Romayne was gazing to the other side of the garden, and it was evidently something she had seen there which had affected her so powerfully. Turning her own curious eyes in the same direction, Hilda Compton saw nothing calculated to account for such an effect. The crowd had drifted away to some extent to the other lawn, and the tennis-courts, and there was a considerable space, sparsely sprinkled with people, between where they stood and the last group on the lawn; a group of ladies to whom the host was introducing a little alert, elderly man with grey hair; a little man who looked to-day—though only one pair of the two pair of women's eyes fixed upon him across the lawn recognised this—exactly as he had looked twenty years ago.

Hilda Compton did not know him, and she was wondering curiously whether Mrs. Romayne did, when she heard their hostess's voice and turned quickly.

Mrs. Romayne, roused apparently by finding herself addressed, had turned also—very quickly it seemed to Hilda Compton, and rather as though she did not wish her face to be seen by some one on the other side of the garden—and was listening with a dazed, strained expression of enforced attention.

"I want to introduce a connexion of mine, my dear Mrs. Romayne. Something of a traveller, and something of an eccentricity; but, really, worth talking to. There he is!" indicating the little alert, elderly man on the other side of the lawn. "He is a Dr. Aston. May I fetch him?"

To Hilda Compton's astonishment Mrs. Romayne stretched out her hand hurriedly in unmistakeable dissent, and it was shaking like a leaf.

"I'm afraid I must say 'no,'" she said, in a hoarse, hurried tone which sounded as though she could hardly control it. "I have a long drive, you know, and I must run away."

She took her leave so briefly and hurriedly that her hostess came to the conclusion that illness must be the cause of the seclusion in which she was living, and that she must have miscalculated her strength that afternoon.

She might have thought so with even more reason if she had seen the strange collapse of her whole figure with which Mrs. Romayne sank back into the corner of her carriage as she was driven home along the country roads. If her attendance at the garden-party had been indeed a desperate attempt at finding some sort of temporary oblivion or distraction, that attempt had obviously failed. Her face was drawn and set, and in her eyes, as they stared unseeingly before her, there was a look as of a woman who is quivering still under the influence of some horrible shock.

She had, as she had said, a long drive home, and as she neared her own house that look in her eyes faded, displaced by a sick hunger of anxiety. She got out of the carriage quickly, helping herself a good deal as she rose, however, as if that shock had affected her physical strength.

"Has Mr. Julian come?" she said to the servant who opened the door; then as the woman answered in the negative, she moved swiftly on to where her letters lay waiting for her, and looked them rapidly over. There was none from Julian, and she carried them listlessly upstairs as she went to dress for her solitary dinner.

The rain, which was falling fast by this time in London, was just beginning to patter slowly on the window when she came into the dining-room; and the wind was rising and moving gustily round the house. They were dreary sounds, both of them, and Mrs. Romayne shivered a little as she sat down. Apparently the monotonous pattering, growing quicker and quicker as dinner went on, or the low howling of the wind, made her nervous. She ate nothing, and when at last, the form of dinner having been gone through with, and the servant having left the room, she rose and walked aimlessly to the fireplace, her lips were strangely compressed, and she seemed to control the expression of her eyes with a determined effort. It was as though she were controlling something within of which the tendency frightened her. She stood there forgetting, apparently, to go into the drawing-room, her face fixed and intent as though she were reasoning or arguing with herself. At last she shivered sharply and her lips twitched. Then rousing herself forcibly, as it seemed, she rang the bell fiercely, and gave orders that a fire should be lighted in the drawing-room. It was a wretched evening, she said to the servant, as though the audible expression of a tangible reason for the nervous discomfort which seemed to be upon her was some sort of relief to her. The fire lighted, she drew a chair in front of it, and taking up a novel, set herself to read with a desperate determination in every line of her face.

Down one page, line by line, on through the next, still line by line, her eyes travelled steadily, mechanically; and then, as mechanically, her hand moved, turned the leaf, and her eyes moved on again. But unless her face greatly belied her, the sense of the words she read so intently never penetrated to her brain. By-and-by that movement of her eyes ceased; she sat staring fixedly at the page before her; then she let the hand that held the book sink gradually on her knee, and sat staring into space as she had sat staring at the printed words. Her face was drawn, and there was an intense, indefinite dread about it which was none the less ghastly in that it would have been impossible to say in which of her set features its shadow lurked.

The room was absolutely still. Outside the rain fell and the wind moaned. Inside the intense quiet seemed to be taking a weirdly tangible form, and to be creeping closer and closer round her motionless figure with every breath she drew.

With a sudden, sharp movement, as though, in taking a too sharply piercing point, her thoughts had roused her to a desperate resistance of them, she rose, and began to walk restlessly up and down the room.

Her brows were drawn to a concentration which made her whole face look thin and very old. There was an expression of deliberate, self-conscious self-contempt about her mouth, but in her eyes there lurked the battling horror against which all her force seemed to be fiercely arrayed. Up and down she walked, no muscle of her set face relaxing; until, quite suddenly, there swept across it, breaking up all its rigid lines, a very agony of yearning. It was as though some sudden and most inopportune realisation, in no wise to be resisted, had shaken her through and through.

"If only I had dared to ask him! If only, if only I dared to speak!"

The words had broken from her half aloud, a sharp, low cry, and as she uttered them she stopped in her walk, gripping and clinging to a chair as if for physical support in a moment of terrible mental conflict. She was evidently fighting desperately inch by inch for the self-control which was slipping from her; the self-control which she dreaded to lose as she dreaded nothing else in life; the self-control to which she clung with the tenacity of instinctive self-preservation.

She lifted her face at last, still and hard as resolution could make it. She crossed the room with quick, resolute steps, looking neither to the right nor the left, and went rapidly upstairs to her own room. A desk containing a quantity of papers stood on the chest of drawers. They were old bills and receipts that needed sorting and destroying, and she had brought them into the country saying that she never had time for such work in town. She went up to this desk now, lifted it in her two hands, and placing it on the table, sat down before it and unlocked it. All her movements were the quick, concentrated movements of a woman to whom employment, close, tedious employment, has become an absolute necessity.

A telegram ten days old was not among the papers to be sorted, but Mrs. Romayne held one in her hand as she sat there at her writing-table. She had drawn it from the front of her dress and she read and re-read it, oblivious of the task she had set herself, with an intensity in her eyes which seemed as though it would wring a hidden meaning from the words. It was the telegram Julian had sent her ten days before. She folded it at last with a quick defiant gesture and drew towards her a packet of receipts.

She untied the string that fastened the papers, and out from among them there fell a folded letter, yellow with age, and crumpled. It had evidently worked its way into that packet by accident, as papers will when many are kept together, for it was obviously a letter and not a bill. Mrs. Romayne stretched out her hand mechanically and picked it up and opened it. Her eyes were met by the words, written in a childish, scrawling, much blotted handwriting: "My dear mamma."

It was the letter which she had received from Julian twenty years ago at Nice.

In an instant, even as her eyes fell on those faded baby characters, so suddenly and so utterly that she never realised her loss, the self-control to which she had clung so fiercely melted away from Mrs. Romayne. Before the flash and quiver of recognition had subsided on her face she had seized the bell-rope and was ringing furiously for her maid. The woman, appearing breathless and alarmed a moment later, found her mistress searching feverishly for bonnet and cloak.

"I am going to London, Dawson. Order the carriage at once."

The voice was harsh, rapid, and peremptory; but the bewildered woman hesitated.

"Now, ma'am?"

Mrs. Romayne turned on her with such a face as her maid had never seen before.

"At once, I said. At once!"

The last train was just steaming into the station when Mrs. Romayne's carriage dashed up, the horse smoking and covered with foam.

She had thrust that yellow little letter half-unconsciously into her pocket, and all through the journey she sat motionless, clasping it tightly in her hand, her eyes wild, her features forced into a quiescence which sat upon them like a mask.

That mask seemed to get thin, to break away now and again, as she drove through the London streets at last, as though the wild emotion which it hid was growing too strong for it. Her breath was coming faster and faster, until her white, parted lips took an involuntary line of physical pain.

There were no lights in the house in Chelsea as her cab drew up. It was twelve o'clock. She rang violently, and waited, her rapid breathing almost suffocating her. No one came. She rang again, pausing this time with her hand on the bell; again and again, furiously, as a wild, unreasoning horror seemed to seize upon her and tear at her heart. At last there was a sound as of the tentative undoing of bolts and turning of keys. The door was opened an inch or two, and a frightened woman's voice said:

"Who is it?"

A moment later there was no possibility of doubt on that score. The door was hurriedly thrown open, and Mrs. Romayne moved swiftly into the hall, turning fiercely to confront the astonished, partially-dressed servant, whose bedroom candle seemed to be the only light in the house.

"Has Mr. Julian gone to bed?" she demanded, and the woman hardly recognised her mistress's voice.

"Mr. Julian is not here, ma'am!" she answered. "He has not been here since the day before yesterday."

CHAPTER XIII

"Mr. Falconer, sir! Mr. Falconer!"

Dennis Falconer was a light sleeper, and he was awake on the first call, low and hurried as it was. It must be a very bad morning, he said to himself, for the light was not nearly so strong as it usually was when he was called at eight o'clock.

"All right!" he called back.

But the retreating footsteps that usually ensued upon his answer did not follow.

"There's a lady, sir, to see you, please. She's waiting in the sitting-room. 'Mrs. Romayne,' she told me to say."

"What!" It was a sharp exclamation of inexpressible astonishment, and as he uttered it Falconer sprang out of bed. As he did so he realised that the unusualness of the light was due to the unusualness of the hour—seven o'clock only. "Some one from Mrs. Romayne, you mean?" he called, his strong, deep voice full of incredulity and apprehension. Then, as the answer came through the door, "'Mrs. Romayne,' sir, the lady said," he called back hurriedly: "Say I will be with her in a moment."

Very few moments indeed had passed before Falconer's bedroom door opened and he came out with a rapid step. He opened his sitting-room door and passed in, shutting the door hastily behind him, and as he did so the words of grave concern with which he had entered died upon his lips.

In the disorder and dreariness of a room from which the traces of yesterday's usage had not yet been obliterated; in the cold grey light of the early September morning; a woman was pacing up and down with almost frenzied steps. For a moment, as he caught his first glimpse of the face, he thought vaguely that it was not Mrs. Romayne; then it turned and confronted him, and, meeting the eyes, he recognised, not the woman whom he had known during the past two years, but the woman into whose face he had looked with so strange a shock of unfamiliarity, and for one moment only, as he and Dr. Aston had confronted it together twenty years ago in Nice. Every trace of the Mrs. Romayne of to-day seemed to have vanished, scorched away by the consuming fire which burnt in her blue eyes and seemed to be the only thing that lived behind that ghastly face; even her features were drawn and sunken almost beyond recognition.

An almost paralysing sense of unreality fell upon Dennis Falconer, for all his practical common sense; and before he could recover himself sufficiently for speech, Mrs. Romayne had crossed the room to him, attempting no greeting, swept away on a tide before which all the barriers of her life—all the safeguards, as they had seemed to her—had gone down in one common ruin.

"Dennis Falconer," she cried hoarsely, "my boy is gone—gone! Help me to think what I must do—help me to think how I can find him! Help me! Help me!"

The words themselves were an appeal, but they rang out in that harsh, untuned voice with all the fierce peremptoriness of a command, and as she spoke them Mrs. Romayne beat her hands one against the other, as though her agony were indeed too great to be endured. Falconer, utterly confounded—more by her manner than by her tidings, which, indeed, in his slow and bewildered sense of the extraordinarily direct communication which her words had established between herself and him, he hardly grasped—echoed the one word which seemed to contain a definite statement.

"Gone?" he said. "Gone?"

"Gone!" she returned, repeating the word as she had done before in a kind of hoarse cry. "Oh, let me try and make you understand clearly, that we may lose no time. Time! Ah! who knows how much may have been lost already? My boy! my boy!"

She strangled the cry in her very throat, and laying one hand on Falconer's arm with a convulsive grip, as if to steady herself, she lifted the other to her head, pushing the hair back from her forehead and pressing her fingers down as though to force herself to think and speak coherently.

"I had a telegram from him," she said, speaking in short, quick sentences with heavy, panting breaths between, "ten days ago. It said that he was going to stop in town for a few days. Yesterday I heard something that made me uneasy. I came up to speak to him late last night. I expected to find him in Queen Anne Street. He was not there. He has not been there for the last two nights. He is gone!" She stopped as though in those three words she had summed up all the horror of the situation; and with that strange sense of unreality making his voice stiff and constrained, Falconer said:

"But must you necessarily apprehend anything alarming? Some private visit, perhaps; a painful discovery, of course——"

She tore her hand away from his arm, wringing it fiercely with its fellow as she faced him, breaking in upon his words with a passionate cry.

"Apprehend! Apprehend! I know, I tell you, I know! Ah! have I been watching and fighting for so many years; have I planned and struggled and sickened with fear; not to know, now that it has overtaken me at last? Dennis Falconer, don't palter with me. You know what lies about my boy. You know what horrible inheritance I have had to battle with for him. Good Heaven!

when have you spared me your knowledge of it? When have you failed to thrust it on me, to force me to shudder and sicken even when I felt most secure?"

She paused, battling for breath; and then, as Falconer tried to speak, she put out her hand to stop him, and went on hurriedly:

"That's all over! It's done with! Now you must help me. Your knowledge must help me. You are a man. You will know what to do; how he can be saved! He must be saved! He must!"

She turned away from him with a wild, unconscious gesture, as though his personality had no existence for her save and except as he could serve her purpose, and began once more to pace up and down the room.

Falconer followed her with his eyes, standing motionless and confounded. The very foundation on which stood his every conception with regard to the woman before him, and the life she lived, had suddenly melted into nothingness before her passionate words, and there seemed for the time being to be no stability anywhere about him. It was no light that her words let in upon him. Rather, they rolled over that mental tract of country which had been to him perfectly familiar and commonplace, a darkness in which every landmark was obliterated. In those first bewildered seconds his most prominent sensation was one of utter blackness—the mental counterpart of the effect produced upon the physical vision by the sudden substitution of illimitable darkness for a narrow and well-known scene.

"What do you fear?" he said. He spoke almost like an automaton, in a low, tentative tone.

"He has been speculating." She never stopped in her rushing walk. "I have known it for months, and I have been in torment." There was a strange, scathed look on her face which gave the words a terrible reality. "He has had some heavy anxiety on his mind all the summer—what, I don't know. But this is the end of it. Oh, my boy, my darling, what have I done that you should shut your mother out? I have slaved for you! I have slaved for you, and I will slave for you as long as I live! Why have you gone away from me?"

She was not crying. To Falconer, watching her and listening to her, no tears could have been so terrible as that bitter, dry-eyed wail which seemed to him to echo in a void, where nothing answering to it could have been nurtured into life. The contrast between the artificial woman he had known hitherto, and the woman in the consuming anguish of her motherhood with whom he now found himself face to face, was so amazing that he could make no attempt to grapple with it. He took desperate and instinctive refuge in the practical.

"Do you know anything of his City associations?" he said.

She made a despairing gesture of negation.

"I did!" she said hoarsely. "I did all I knew to keep in touch with him. Two months ago Marston Loring could have told me anything. But everything failed me! Everything crumbled away! They quarrelled."

Already, with that matter-of-fact tendency inherent in all men—and particularly in unimaginative men—which assimilates a revelation, and reduces it involuntarily to a commonplace, Falconer had become almost accustomed to the new point of view which had been forced upon him. The darkness was lifting, and he was aware of vast tracts of mental country, destitute of those landmarks which his soul loved, but no longer enveloped in a dense atmosphere of confusion.

A man of Falconer's narrow temperament, confirmed in his rigidity by many years of life, having his set conceptions suddenly overthrown and forcibly enlarged, will be totally incapable of any just appreciation of the new horizon then created; he will be conscious of the spaces about him only as confusing unrealities; the limitations solidified by the mental habits of years will retain some sort of ghostly influence over him long after they have ceased to have any actual existence. His first conscious and deliberate movement will be an instinctive attempt to reconcile the new condition of things with these old limitations, rather than to reconcile himself with the new conditions. The facts which Mrs. Romayne's words recalled to him; the character of the man whom she had encouraged as her son's chief intimate; the character of the life to which she had bred him; gave definite force to the vague movement towards such reconciliation already stirring in Falconer's mind. He accepted the revelation of unsuspected mother's love and mother's dread, and ceased to contemplate it as he concentrated his mental vision on the selfish vanity and worldliness with which Mrs. Romayne had stood endued in his thoughts for twenty years; and as his point of view readjusted itself on these lines, her present position, with all the suffering which it involved, presented itself to him solely as the inevitable climax of a simple and eminently comprehensible sequence of cause and effect.

His voice was low and stern as he said:

"Can you not think of any other friend who could give us some clue to his recent movements?"

"I can't!" she cried, stopping in her rapid walk, and confronting him fiercely. "It is because there is no one left; because I don't know what to do, or where to turn, that I have come to you! Should I be wasting time like this if I could think of any other means of acting? I'm tied hand and foot in the dark—tied to the rack, man! We can do nothing till we find him—till we know what has happened. Think, think, think! How are we to find him? How are we to——"

Her voice, which had risen into an agonised cry, broke suddenly; a greyish tint spread itself over her face, and all her features were contorted as if with horrible physical pain. She stretched out her hand feebly and gropingly, caught at an arm-chair, and fell into it, letting her face fall forward on its back as her nails pressed themselves pitilessly into her thin hands.

"It—it's nothing!" she gasped, in a tight, suppressed voice, fighting desperately, as it seemed, to utter words rather than groans. "I have been ill! The night——"

The words died away, caught and strangled by the relentless, stabbing pain, and Falconer, utterly at a loss, stood for a moment helplessly watching her, and then strode across the room meaning to call a woman to his aid. He opened the door hurriedly and then stopped short. On the shelf fixed against the wall facing him there lay his morning letters, and on the top of the pile lay one directed in Julian's handwriting. Mrs. Romayne's physical distress sank into insignificance for him. The physical suffering which had fallen to his lot during the past year had by no means obliterated the lifelong instinct which led him to look upon such weakness as a detail to be disregarded, and of women he knew nothing. He turned back into the room with the letter in his hand, and shutting the door again opened it hastily. It was the letter Julian had written on the previous day in his room in the Temple.

"DEAR FALCONER," he read,—"I've done for myself all round, and by the time you get this I shall be out of England. It's penal servitude if I stay. The smash will come in a day or two and you will understand. It's all up with me; but there's my wife and child—for Heaven's sake be kind to them. This is the address." The address followed, and then the signature.

For another moment Dennis Falconer stood motionless with his eyes fixed on the letter, so despairing in its hopeless brevity, so terribly eloquent of immeasurable disgrace and wrong. Then he lifted his head and turned towards Mrs. Romayne. She had not moved, she was apparently unconscious of his presence; the tense rigidity of her position had passed into a total collapse, in which all her figure seemed to have fallen together as if in absolute exhaustion. To Falconer she presented an appearance only of most desirable quiet, and he hesitated simply as to how he should so break to her what must be broken, as to excite her least. She would have to see the letter! He glanced at it again on the thought, and a cold shock seemed to strike him as he realised the total oblivion of his mother to which the young man's last appeal bore witness.

"I have received some news," he said.

His tone, as he spoke, was curiously different from any in which he had ever before addressed her. It was grave, straightforward, and not unkindly, and it very subtly—and quite unconsciously—conveyed the altered attitude of a stern and narrow moralist towards wrong-doing, no longer triumphant and serene, but writhing under its merited suffering. A certain stern compassion the new position of affairs demanded of him, and he gave it; but it was that lofty compassion which is more than half composed of a sense of the righteousness of the retribution meted out; with sympathy or respect it was utterly untouched. He was prepared to help her to the utmost; he was steady reliability itself; but his help was permeated, as was his compassion, with a superior recognition of the justice of the trouble which rendered that help necessary.

As though there was something between her and her surroundings through which his voice must penetrate before it reached her brain, a second or two elapsed before Mrs. Romayne gave any sign of having heard him. Then she moved and turned her face towards him, looking at him as though from a long way off. Her forehead and the hair about it, strangely colourless and dead-looking, were damp. Grey shadows had fallen about her mouth. There was a faint struggle in her dull eyes, as though she had heard his words and was trying to force her way to an understanding of them through overwhelming physical disabilities.

"I am sorry to say it is far from reassuring," continued Falconer.

A sudden flash of understanding and conviction flashed across her features, and its spirit dominated her weakness as its light transfigured her face. She rose, clinging to the chair, but evidently absolutely unconscious of any physical sensation, and held out her hand, still clammy and tremulous with pain.

"Give it me," she said, indicating the letter he held. Her voice was a thin whisper. Then, as he hesitated: "You're wasting time. Give it me."

He gave it her without a word and turned away. It would break her down, of course, he thought; perhaps into some wild form of hysteria at the position in which the young man confessed himself; perhaps into passionate repudiation of the son who had so deceived her, and who was leaving her without word or sign. Moments passed, three or four perhaps, and then a tense, insistent touch fell on his arm and he turned. Mrs. Romayne was standing by his side, Julian's letter held tightly in her hand, which trembled no longer. Her eyes were bright, almost hard in their determination, and every line and muscle of her face and figure was braced and set into a vivid strength and resolution.

"We must see this woman at once," she said, and her voice was as strange in its desperate energy as was her face. Then, as Falconer only looked at her blankly, she added, in the same absorbed, concentrated way: "You will come with me?"

"You mean you will see——"

"I must see this woman," she repeated, tapping the paper impatiently with her hand. "Don't you see she will probably know where he is? She must know! Let us go at once!"

"But if she does know?"

"If she does know! Why, that is everything! I can follow him. He is frightened—he has lost his head. If he goes away like this he is lost. I am going to stop him."

"But——"

She silenced him with a movement of her hand, before which his words died on his lips.

"Dennis Falconer," she said, "help me or refuse to help me as you like, but don't try to stop me. The shadow of a horror such as this has haunted me for twenty years. I bring the nerve and desperation of twenty years to meet it now, and I am going to save him. Will you come?"

Dominated against his will, sternly disapproving, but powerless to assert his disapprobation in the face of the intensity of her determination, Falconer made a slight gesture of enforced assent. Mrs. Romayne hardly waited for it before she turned and went swiftly out of the room and down the stairs.

It was early still—not yet eight o'clock—and cabs were hardly to be found. They met one at last, and Falconer put her into it and looked at her, obviously with an intention of uttering the protest with which his face was full. She made a peremptory sign that he should give the address, holding out the letter containing it, and instantly reclaiming it. Her nerves were evidently strung beyond the possibility of irrelevant or unnecessary speech. A long drive followed to a dingy, poverty-stricken neighbourhood, and then, in a dreary-looking little street, the cab stopped. Mrs. Romayne got out with the same rapid, concentrated movements, signing again, with a movement of her set lips, to Falconer that he should ring and make the necessary enquiries. The bell was answered, after an appreciable interval, by a slatternly-looking girl.

"A young woman lodges here, I believe," said Falconer sternly—"a young married woman. Mrs.—Mrs. Roden, or Romayne?"

The girl stared at him for a moment with bold, curious eyes, and then transferred the stare to Mrs. Romayne, with a coarse giggle.

"Young married woman?" she repeated, with a toss of the head. "Oh, yes; of course! Top floor back!"

Before the last words, which conveyed a general intimation that visitors for the top floor back were expected to show themselves up, were well uttered, Mrs. Romayne had crossed the dirty little passage with swift steps and was mounting the stairs. She went straight on until she reached the top landing, and then she turned sharply to Falconer, who had followed her closely. His judgement condemned her proceedings utterly, but his stern sense of her claim upon him remained untouched, and he believed himself to be merely waiting until her impulse should fail her, as it seemed to him it must before long, to take matters into his own hands.

"Knock!" she said.

Falconer obeyed her; the door was opened with a quiet, sad-toned "Yes?" and Clemence stood on the threshold.

She was looking very fragile and very white; the haggard look of suffering had left her, but it had taken with it in the passing all the physical strength from her face. Her eyes were heavy as with sleeplessness and tears, and from their depths there seemed to emanate the quiet grief which spoke in every line of her face. She held her baby in her arms, and her whole personality seemed to be touched by the mysterious influence of motherhood into a new dignity and beauty. To Falconer the change in her since he had seen her in Camden Town was so great as to give him a moment's absolute shock; it was the same woman, and yet not the same. The difference lay, for him, rather in the evidences of long suffering which spoke so eloquently about that woman's face and form, than in the work effected by that suffering; and the feeling that the sight of her stirred in him was one of pity; a man's half indignant, half patronising pity for weakness and trust abused.

But Falconer she did not seem to see. Instantly, as she opened the door, her eyes had passed to where Mrs. Romayne stood confronting her, her face absorbed, concentrated, hard as steel. A faint flush of colour flooded Clemence's face; then she lowered her eyes, and stood with her head a little bent over her child, motionless.

"You are my son's wife?"

The words came from Mrs. Romayne quick, terse, utterly untouched and unemotional, as though the situation in itself were absolutely devoid of meaning for her.

"My husband's name is Julian Romayne," was the low answer.

Mrs. Romayne made a quick, imperious gesture indicative of her desire to pass into the little room, on the threshold of which Clemence was standing. Clemence made way for her with quiet dignity, and then followed her in. Falconer hesitated an instant and took up his position in the doorway, holding himself in grave, attentive readiness until the moment when his presence should be required. The little room was scrupulously neat and clean. Facing him, a strangely incongruous figure amid such poor surroundings, but apparently as absolutely unconscious of them as of the child—at which she never glanced—stood Mrs. Romayne. Facing Mrs. Romayne stood Clemence, paler now than before, and with her head bent a little lower. Falconer could see that she trembled slightly. Mrs. Romayne began to speak instantly, in the same hard, rapid tone.

"Where is my son?" she said. "You have been told, perhaps, to say you do not know—to keep his plans secret. You must give them up instantly to me. He has made a mistake, and only prompt action can redeem it. When did you see him last? What did he tell you?"

As though some subtle influence from the one woman had penetrated to the heart of the other, Clemence's face had turned quite white. For her, too, the personal aspect of the situation seemed suddenly to sink into abeyance. Her head was lifted, and her eyes, filled with a creeping apprehension, were fixed full upon Mrs. Romayne, oblivious of anything but the one interest which they held in common.

The man watching them was vaguely conscious of something about the two women which put him quite away from them; which made him the merest spectator of something to which he had no key.

"I saw him last night," said Clemence, hurriedly and fearfully; "he came to say good-bye!"

A kind of hoarse cry broke from Mrs. Romayne.

"Good-bye!" she cried, as though appealing to some encircling environment of fate. "And she let him go! She let him go!" She stopped herself, forcing down her passion with an iron hand, and went on in a tone only colder and more decisive in its greater rapidity than before. "He has made a mistake; you cannot understand, of course. No doubt it seems to you that everything to be desired is comprised in the miserable subterfuge of flight. No doubt——"

She was interrupted. With a low cry of unutterable horror Clemence had drawn a step nearer to her, pressing her baby passionately to her heart.

"Flight!" she cried. "Flight! Ah, I knew! I knew there was something wrong! What is it? Oh, what is it? My dear, my dear, what have you done? What have you done?"

There was an instant's dead silence as the cry died away and Clemence stood with her beseeching eyes dark and dilated, her uplifted face white and quivering, appealing, as it seemed, for an answer, to Julian himself. Falconer was looking straight before him, his face set and grim, passive, not only with the natural passivity of a man in the presence of inevitable anguish, but with the involuntary self-forgetfulness of a man in the presence of a power greater than he can understand. Mrs. Romayne had paused as though stopped by some kind of hard, annoyed surprise.

Then Mrs. Romayne went on in a thin, tense voice:

"There is no time to waste over what has been done; the point is to retrieve it! He must come back at once. Where is he?"

With a sudden quick movement Clemence turned, crossed the room, and laid the child tenderly in the little cot standing by the fire. She pressed her face down for one instant to the tiny sleep-flushed cheek, and then rose and came back to Mrs. Romayne and Falconer, her face white and resolute, her eyes shining, glancing from one to the other as she spoke.

"Will there be time?" she said. "Can I get to him before he sails? There is a woman downstairs who will take care of my child. He is alone! He may be doing——Flight! What can flight do for him if he has done wrong? He doesn't always know! I am his wife, and I must go and help him. Will there be time?"

It was Falconer to whom her eyes finally turned, vaguely conscious of the absence of womanly sympathy, and appealing in the void for a man's knowledge and assistance. It was Falconer who answered her. Instinctively and involuntarily he answered her directly, the current of his thoughts seeming to submit itself to hers without an impulse to resist or control her.

"Where was he going?" he said.

"To America!" was the answer, eager and low, as though life and death hung on the response it should elicit. "He was going then, he told me. That was at nine o'clock last night! Oh, if I go at once I shall be in time? I shall be in time?"

A hard, nervous irritation was disturbing the concentration of Mrs. Romayne's face. Futile and utterly to be ignored as seemed to her any impulse on the part of the woman to whom, in the face of the terrible issues with which she stood confronted, she gave no personal consideration whatever; the introduction of such futility seemed, in the strained, tense condition of her nerves, to involve irrelevancy and delay, which she was utterly unable to meet with any self-command. She broke in now, her voice harsh and vibrating with uncontrollable impatience.

"There is no need," she said. "I am on my way to him now. You—there is no need for you! You can do nothing!"

"I am his wife!" said Clemence.

She did not raise her voice; no colour came to her dead, white face; only she turned to Julian's mother, with her hands crushed tightly together against her heart, and such a light shining in her eyes as seemed to transfigure her whole face and figure. For an instant the eyes of the two women met and held one another. Then Mrs. Romayne, with a gesture which seemed to repudiate and deny the influence which nevertheless she was powerless to resist, turned to Falconer and moved swiftly towards the door. "What does it matter?" she said, in a tone of fierce impatience, which relegated Clemence to the position of the merest nonentity. "The only thing of consequence is time!"

She swept out of the room as she spoke, and Clemence turned again to Falconer, stretching out beseeching hands.

"Help me!" she said.

The movement which he had thought to guide and control so easily had passed beyond Falconer's control, and he knew it. He could only follow it, waiting until the turn of events should throw it, as he still believed they must, upon a man's strength and experience. But as Clemence had touched him once before against his will, she touched him now against his judgement, and he answered her in one word:

"Come!"

Throughout the terrible hours that followed; during the drive to the station, the sickening suspense, the brief interval of waiting for a train, the long journey; neither by word nor sign did Mrs. Romayne evince the slightest consciousness of Clemence's presence. Her face, almost stony now in its set determination, never altered. After they were seated in the train she never spoke at all. She sat gazing straight before her, motionless as a statue, like a woman living only by her hold upon a moment in the future, to which each present second as it passed was bringing her nearer.

There had been no time to ascertain the probabilities as to their forestalling the sailing of the boat in which Julian had presumably intended to leave England. Falconer, while admitting to himself that the young man might have over-estimated, panic-stricken, the danger in which he had placed himself, had but faint hope that any steps other than the promotion of his speedy departure would be possible when they should be in possession of the facts; even should their arrival be in time to frustrate his original determination. But Mrs. Romayne weighed no probabilities. She looked neither to the right nor to the left. She saw before her only the climax and consummation of the struggle of twenty years, and on that consummation was concentrated her whole existence.

CHAPTER XIV

THE room was very still; even the clock upon the mantelpiece was not going, so that not even a low tick disturbed the perfect quiet. It was a sitting-room in one of the Liverpool hotels, and quite alone in it was Clemence. She was sitting near the window, motionless, her hands clasped tightly together on her knee. Her face was lifted slightly towards the sky, and its calm, broken now and again by a slight quiver of the lips, was that of intense absorption. Clemence's was one of those natures in which great mental suffering of any kind passes instinctively into unformed prayer; and she was praying now with her whole being, with no faintest consciousness of herself or her mental attitude.

She had been sitting there alone and motionless for more than an hour, when a touch fell upon the handle of the door. She started violently, and rose involuntarily to her feet as it opened to admit Falconer. She did not speak; all her agony of questioning seemed to have passed into the eyes she fixed upon him, and into those tightly-clasped hands.

Falconer crossed the room quickly to her, and spoke as though in answer to audible words.

"I have found him!" he said. "There has been some delay. The boat will not leave until to-morrow, and till then he is here."

A breath of unutterable relief and thanksgiving broke from Clemence's white lips, and she let her face fall forward for a moment on her hands. Then she lifted it again, tremulous and shaken. "Is it—right—that he should go?" she said.

"It is necessary!" returned Falconer sternly. But the sternness was not for her.

A look of trouble and perplexity passed into her face; her lips were parted to speak again when a door at the other end of the room opened sharply—not the door by which Falconer had entered, but a second, leading, presumably, into a bedroom—and Mrs. Romayne appeared. The rigidity of her self-control had given place, apparently, to a consuming fever. Her eyes were glittering, the dry skin seemed to be too tightly drawn across her sharpened features. There was no paint upon her now—no mask, less tangible but no less effective, of artificiality of expression. It was the very woman, stripped of all the trappings of her life, bearing the ravages of past struggles thick upon her, driven to bay, and braced to hold the struggle on which she was entering with the last breath in her body. She was still dressed for walking, and the contrast between the smart, somewhat youthful, apparel which she had always affected, and her face, was terrible to see.

She came straight up to Falconer, utterly unconscious, apparently, as far as feeling and realisation constitute consciousness, of Clemence's presence. "You have found him?" she said, and the words were less a question than an assertion. "Let us go at once. Stop, though!" she added abruptly, laying a burning hand on Falconer's arm, as though in the haste and pressure of her own impulses she ascribed a similar impatience to him. "I had better know the facts first. What has he told you?"

Falconer hesitated. His words, when he spoke, ignored her final question, and answered the idea which vibrated behind every word of her speech. He glanced at Clemence as he began to speak as though he wished his words to apply to her also.

"I do not think," he said, "that anything will be gained by your seeing him—except extreme distress for all concerned. I fear there is nothing to be done!"

He had spoken very firmly, as though the moment had arrived, in his estimation, for that stand on manly judgement which he had involuntarily postponed for so long; and he paused as though to accentuate the weight of his words.

Mrs. Romayne, with a gesture of irrepressible, tortured impatience, but otherwise with no recognition whatever of his having spoken, repeated her question:

"What has he told you?"

Clemence's eyes, fixed upon Falconer's face, dilated slightly, and then the shadow of a smile touched her parted lips.

"I fear there is no doubt that it is a bad affair," continued Falconer. "There are forged documents connected with it, and misappropriation of money fraudulently come by; and detection seems to be inevitable. His only hope of safety lies in flight."

As though with the very tangibility and imminence of the danger she had come forth to meet Mrs. Romayne's spirit rose higher, the only sort of change brought to her face by the words was an intensifying of all its previous characteristics of growing courage and determination. From Clemence's lips the little tremulous light had died, quenched in such a horror of vicarious shame, of pity, love, and anguish unspeakable, as seemed to freeze her where she stood.

"The facts! The facts!" The words came from Mrs. Romayne sharp and tense, seeming to put aside and ignore any extraneous comment or opinion.

Falconer hesitated again for a moment and scanned her face closely, absolutely unconscious of his own incapacity for reading what was written there. So far was he from an adequate conception of the realities of the situation, that he thought that a plain statement of details would crush out for ever the hope of which he was conscious in her. And he decided that such instantaneous crushing was the only mercy he could show her.

Gravely and concisely, with no unnecessary comment, he told her the whole story as he had gathered it half an hour earlier from Julian's incoherent, despairing words. He finished and paused, holding himself braced for the outbreak of despair which he expected.

His words were followed by a dead silence. His eyes were fixed on Mrs. Romayne with a vague fear for her reason, and he felt rather than saw that Clemence had turned away and was standing with her face hidden in her hands. Mrs. Romayne's brows had contracted as if in intense thought, and her eyes were extraordinarily bright and keen. At last, with no slightest relaxation of the intent calculation of her face, she asked one or two questions as to details of business procedure, the words coming from her sharp and distinct; questions of which Falconer, as he answered them, tried in vain to see the drift. Then she moved with a gesture of determination, so self-absorbed that it seemed to isolate her utterly.

"Take me to him at once!" she said.

A sharp exclamation broke from Falconer, and, as she moved towards the door, he followed her hastily, indescribably disturbed and confused by so entirely unexpected a course of action.

"To what purpose?" he said quickly. "I beg of you to be advised by me. The boy must go! Nothing can be gained but a parting——"

Mrs. Romayne turned upon him and faced him suddenly.

"I am here to see my son," she said, and there was something in her voice—rather in what its intense restraint suggested than in its tones themselves—absolutely dominating and conclusive. "You came to help me. Take me to him, or tell me where to find him."

Intensely annoyed and disapproving; keenly alive to the fear that Julian, so taken by surprise, might impute to him some definitely treacherous intention in withholding, as he had done, the fact that he was not alone; Falconer yet felt himself powerless. He had no shadow of a right to stand between mother and son. He had made his stand, and he might as effectually have opposed himself to the wind. His words, his judgement, were as nothing to her. That he should so far fail to carry into effect his conception of his duty as her escort, as to let her go alone was, of course, impossible in his eyes. He made a sternly unwilling sign to the effect that he would perforce accompany her, and then, as she passed quickly out of the room, he looked at Clemence. There was a stunned look upon her face now; she did not even glance at him in answer, but she moved mechanically, as it seemed, and like a woman walking in her sleep, and followed Mrs. Romayne.

Not one word was spoken by either of the trio until they stood, a quarter of an hour later, before a rather dingy door in a dreary passage of an unpretentious and obscure private hotel. Then Falconer spoke in a low, stern tone.

"Here!" he said, indicating the door before them.

Mrs. Romayne moved swiftly forward and turned the handle. For one instant, as the door opened, there was a vision of a dull, bare little sitting-room, touched with a strange glory by a red ray from the setting sun, which slanted right across it; and in the middle of the room, in the full light of that red ray, which fell with an almost weird effect of irradiation upon his attitude of despair, Julian sitting by the table, his head buried on his outstretched arms. For an instant only the picture was visible; then Julian turned his head sharply and sprang to his feet with a cry. His mother was advancing rapidly towards him, but it was not his mother that he saw. It was the figure behind her with the dazed white face all breaking up now into quivering lines. It was to that figure that he stretched out his hands with the hoarse, heart-broken sob:

"Clemmie! Clemmie! They've told you!"

Before the words were uttered, Clemence had rushed past Mrs. Romayne, and was clinging to him in such a sudden agony of sobs and tears as seemed to rend her very heart.

Mrs. Romayne stopped abruptly. Falconer, who was close to her with his back to the door which he had shut swiftly on Julian's cry, saw a spasm of pain cut across the concentration of her face for an instant; and in the flash of anger and impatience which succeeded it, she seemed to recognise Clemence's presence practically for the first time. She fell back a step or two, waiting with contemptuous self-control, her eyes fixed upon the pair before her as they clung together, and Julian tried brokenly and despairingly to soothe the pitiful abandonment of grief with which Clemence was shaken. His own distress increased with every incoherent word of self-reproach he uttered; and it was a sense of his anguish that seemed, at last, to reach Clemence, and produce in her a woman's instinct towards the suppression of her own pain. She disengaged herself gently, forcing back the heavy sob that trembled on her lips, and looked from Julian towards Mrs. Romayne with a tacit recognition of his mother's claims which was as beautiful as it was instinctive.

"You will listen!" she said in a choked, beseeching voice, "you will listen and come back!"

She turned away as she spoke, making him a sign that he should not speak to her; and as she drew away from him Mrs. Romayne advanced rapidly, every movement, every line of her face, every tone of her voice, claiming as an inalienable right her son's attention. Her face was very hard, far harder than it had been before that spasm of pain had shaken it, and there was no touch of emotion in her hard, quick voice. She seemed to have put all sentiment deliberately aside.

"Julian," she said, "you have made a terrible mistake! You are taking just the one false step that would be absolutely irretrievable. You must come back to town at once!"

Her manner; her voice; some influence from the long past days when her word, for all her affectation of weak indulgence, had been his law; had arrested his attention almost without his own consent. He stood now looking at her; looking at her across such a gulf of ignorance, mistake, and wrong as had swallowed even that bitterness with which he had once regarded her, leaving him absolutely cold and dead to her.

"Town and I have parted company, mother!" he said. He spoke hoarsely, but the emotion in his tone was the reflex of that through which he had just passed in meeting Clemence; his manner was even callous.

"That would be true indeed," was the quick answer, "if you had succeeded in leaving England! Not only town and you, but life and you—everything that makes life worth living—would have parted company! To go away now is to cut your own throat!"

Julian turned to Falconer.

"Haven't you told them?" he said thickly. "Don't they know that—that is done?"

Falconer drew a step nearer.

"Your mother knows——" he began; but Mrs. Romayne interposed, lifting her hand peremptorily without even glancing at him.

"I know everything," she said. "I know that you are in hideous danger, and if you run away from it it is indeed all over with you. You must face it; you must defy it!"

As though in her last words she had touched and given form and life to the very core of the determination which had nerved her since she had first read Julian's letter that morning, her voice rose as she spoke them into a ring of indomitable courage, vibrating with the very triumph of that defiance of which she spoke. Her slight, haggard physique seemed to expand, to gain in dignity and power; as the whole room seemed to fill with the magnetism of her intense resolution. There was an instant's pause, and then an exclamation broke alike from Julian and from Falconer. Julian's was almost derisive in its absolute repudiation of her words; Falconer's was sternly incredulous. Clemence was standing a little apart. No sound came from her, but she lifted her face suddenly and turned it towards Mrs. Romayne. A vague horror and confusion had dawned in her eyes.

Before the annihilating words with which Falconer obviously intended to follow up his first ejaculation could be uttered, Mrs. Romayne was speaking again—in a rapid, businesslike tone now, but always with that ring of triumph behind it.

"You must come back with me to-night and take up your position as if nothing could shake it. You must fight for your credit and your social status tooth and nail. When you have lost them you have lost everything! You have not lost them yet, and no risk is too great to run for their retention."

"Not penal servitude?" asked Julian, with a ghastly smile.

"Not penal servitude, not hanging—if that were the risk," returned his mother passionately. "What are you better off if you escape—disgraced, ostracised, ruined beyond all hope of reclamation—than you would be in a convict's cell? What would you have to live for—to hope for? When you have lost your position with the world you have lost everything. What does it matter that you go down in one wave rather than another?" She paused a moment, battling with her fierce horror and repulsion. Then she went on again in another tone, eager and decided. "But the risk is not so frightful after all," she said. "Show it a bold front and we shall triumph over it! Now, listen to me, Julian. This other man—this man Ramsay—was the actual forger?"

She paused for an answer, and apparently the insistence of her tone forced one from Julian in spite of himself.

"As far as the actual commission of the forgery goes—yes," he said sullenly. "But——"

"Then what is there to prove—to prove, mind—that you were a party to it?"

Julian glanced round at Clemence as if involuntarily. Then he looked recklessly back at his mother and laughed harshly.

"The facts——" he began.

His mother caught up the words.

"The facts? Yes!" she said. "But if the facts are denied? Can they be proved? If you face this meeting and say that you yourself have been deceived? Even if it should come to a prosecution there are always loopholes! With good counsel and facing it out ourselves unflinchingly, you would come through untouched! It is the only chance, Julian, and we must dare it."

CHAPTER XV

THE red glow from the setting sun had shifted a little. It fell now behind Julian and between him and Clemence, and its light seemed to isolate the mother and son, shutting them in alone together. Mrs. Romayne stood a few paces from Julian, not touching him or appealing to him, concentrating all her forces on the dominating of his weaker nature. Julian stood doggedly before her, his hands clenched, his face set. Near the window, looking across the shabby little room from which those two figures, eloquent of struggle and crisis, stood out so strangely, was Clemence; her eyes fixed upon Julian now as though life and death hung on his looks. Aloof alike from Clemence and from the mother and son, a grim spectator holding in reserve his weight of condemnation until the upshot of the scene should declare itself, was Dennis Falconer.

For all answer, as though her ringing words had touched him so little that he found them not even worth the trouble of an articulate denial, Julian shook his head sullenly. The gesture witnessed to a heavy dead weight of dissent likely to be more difficult to act upon than the most vehement opposition, and Mrs. Romayne paused for a moment, looking at him, her lips taking a firmer line, her eyes flashing.

"You don't realise the position," she said. "Look at it and understand the choice before you. On the one hand is ignominy, ruin, the end of your career; to reach it you have only to give way to your nerves, to act under the influence of panic, to run away, in short. On the other hand," she moved a step nearer to him with a tense, emphatic gesture, which seemed an outlet for some of the passionate urgency which she was keeping resolutely in hand; "on the other hand is the very reverse of all this. Social position, consideration, the prosperous life to which you have always looked forward—all this is to be retained by one bold stroke, by a little courage and resolution, and at the risk of what is by no means worse than the life which must inevitably be yours if you do not nerve yourself to run it. Julian, think what is at stake!"

Falconer's eyes had been fixed on Mrs. Romayne, severe, inexorable in their condemnation. They travelled, now, to Julian.

Again Julian made that dull gesture of negation.

"It's all over," he said doggedly. "I've staked and lost."

"You have not lost—yet," his mother cried; the vibration in her voice was stronger now, and there were white patches coming and going faintly about her mouth. "You shall not lose while I can lift a hand to save you. Think!—think! It's all before you still—happiness, success, life! You've only to grasp them instead of letting go. Think!"

Julian had been standing with his haggard young face averted from her, staring sullenly at the ground. He turned upon her suddenly, his face quivering with an impotent misery of regret, his voice ringing with hopeless bitterness.

"They're gone," he said. "I've thrown them all away. I might as well be dead, that's true enough. It might be possible to brazen it out—I don't know, I don't care! It wouldn't give me anything worth having. Social position, credit, standing! What good would they be to me? I'm sick of the whole thing! I've done with it!"

His incoherent, hardly articulated words stopped abruptly, and he seemed to struggle fiercely for means of expression; so fiercely that the blind, impotent wrestle with the limitations of a lifetime seemed to dominate the situation for the moment, and in Mrs. Romayne's agonised face, as she watched him, the life seemed arrested. It was as though he were groping and fighting among sensations and instincts so new to him that he had no words in his vocabulary in which to clothe them; and the effort to express them was instinct with the despair of conscious futility. He seemed to break away at last and rush upon a wild, confused declaration which comprised all that he could grasp.

"Why should I fight for what I don't want?" he cried hoarsely. "There's nothing worth having now."

"My boy!" The cry arrested Clemence, moving towards Julian with shining eyes and white, parted lips. It arrested Falconer, who had drawn nearer to Mrs. Romayne, with a desperate impulse to end the struggle by throwing into the scale, against Mrs. Romayne, the weight of his opinion. "My boy, my boy! don't talk like that, for Heaven's sake! For Heaven's sake! Julian, my darling, if not for yourself, for your mother! I have lived for you. I have had no thought in life but you—to save you, to protect you, to keep you from ruin such as this! Don't break my heart. Ah!" she broke into a low, wailing moan, wringing her hands together as her eyes fastened on his face, transfixed into an expression of blank surprise as his eyes met hers for the first time. "Don't look like that! Julian, Julian! In all these years have you never understood? Have you never understood how I have loved you?"

They were face to face, mother and son, all the artificialities and conventionalities of their lives scorched and burnt away. But between them lay that unbridgeable gulf of ignorance and wrong, and her outstretched hands appealed to him in vain. He looked at her coldly, uncertainly, as though she were a stranger to him.

Then, with one strange, gasping cry, she seemed to thrust all consciousness of herself fiercely on one side in her realisation of his great need. In the very crisis of her agony, in the very crisis as it seemed of her defeat, there came upon her a great dignity.

"My son," she said, "there is something in your life of which you have never known—something which accident might have revealed to you at any time, but which I kept from you, hoping that fortune might favour me—as it has done—and preserve your ignorance; believing that in happiness and self-respect lay one of your safeguards, and dreading that knowledge might bring to you some sort of morbid temptation. Julian, it is the toil and struggle of twenty years that you are trampling on in throwing down your life like this. Twenty years ago your father died by his own hand—a swindler, liar, and thief. A few chance words brought home to me the possibility that some such dreadful taint might rest on you. To keep you from its awful consequence; to give you such a life as should obviate the possibility of temptation; to hedge you in with every security that money and position could create for you; to give you such a standing in the world as should leave you nothing to wish for; has been the one thought, the one motive of my life from that time until now."

The speech—so terrible a declaration of a struggle foredoomed by its own essence to failure, a struggle in which the foe was real, the combatant in desperate earnest, and the weapons straws—trembled into an abrupt, palpitating silence, as though her feelings were too intense for speech. There was a moment's stillness like the stillness of death; a stillness broken only by Julian's long, laboured breaths as he stood facing her, his face blanched and frozen into an image of horror. Then he spoke.

"Is it true?" He had turned mechanically to Dennis Falconer, and the words came from him in a hoarse whisper.

Dennis Falconer was white to the lips. Far down in his nature, at the root of the rigid and conventional morality by which he lived, was a pulse which palpitated in harmony with the divine realities of life. And, as like answers to like, that pulse in him had recognised its counterpart at last, through all the cramped distortion that had concealed it for so long, beating full and strong, instinct with the throbbing life of the same great realities, in a dwarfed and darkened woman's soul. Perfect mother love, absolute self-abnegation, let them clothe themselves in what mistaken form they may, are an earnest of ideal love and beauty, and in their presence condemnation must give place to reverence. Conscious, for the first time in his life, that he stood in the midst of that which was beyond his power to analyse or to estimate, he made no attempt at speech. He bowed his head in silence.

Julian looked at him for a moment longer, and then he turned his face once more upon his mother. As though what she saw there struck into her very heart, a cry of pity and tenderness broke from her. She moved swiftly to him, putting her arms about him, trying to draw him into her embrace as though he had been once more her little child.

"Julian!" she cried, "my boy! my boy! Try to understand—try to understand why I have told you this now! I don't ask you to think of me—to think what such a repetition of the past as threatens me in you would be to me—a blow infinitely heavier, an agony infinitely crueller than what came upon me twenty years ago, because of the long struggle to which it would bring defeat, because of the long hope and resolution which it would take out of my heart, because of my love for you, my darling—my darling!" She was kissing his hands now passionately, with that oblivion of any other presence in the room which she had evinced throughout; and Falconer, watching her, fascinated, almost awestruck, saw her, as she went on, lift one of the young man's hands and press it to her cheek, stroking it with a wild, nervous movement of her own thin fingers.

"But there's a motive power for you in it, Julian! A lever for your own pride, your own strength of will. You are panic-stricken, unnerved, worn out. Danger is new to you, my darling! Look at your father's fate—wholesale ruin, disgrace, and obloquy—and let it nerve you to turn away from it. Look down the precipice on the brink of which you are standing, and lay firm hold upon the only rope that can save you. Take your courage in both hands, and we will face the danger and conquer together. Oh, my boy, if it is a hot fire to pass through it won't last long! It leads to safety, to firmer standing-ground, to a new lease of life!"

She was clinging to him convulsively, touching his hands, his hair, his face, as though speech alone afforded an all-insufficient outlet for her agonised beseeching. And as she spoke the last words he seized her hands in his and thrust her from him, not with any personal roughness, but rather unconsciously and involuntarily as in the very isolation of despair.

"Life!" he cried. "What can life give to me beyond what I've got already? I've got my billet! Like father like son! I'm bound for the dogs sooner or later, and I don't care to spin out the journey. Who's going to fight against his fate?"

"It is not fate."

Through that little room, across and above the passion and despair that filled it, the words rang out strong and clear, and Julian turned with a convulsive start to meet them.

Clemence had come swiftly across the room and was standing beside him, facing him as he turned to her; facing Falconer, arrested in a quick movement to interpose, blindly and instinctively as it seemed, between Julian and his mother; facing Mrs. Romayne, as she stood leaning heavily on the back of a chair, her eyes strained and terrible to see, her face ghastly. All that humanity can touch of the beautiful and the inspiring; all the burning faith; the quivering personal realisation of that unseen of which each man is a part; the human love acting upon and reacted on by the divine instinct; was shining out from Clemence's face. She paused hardly for an instant as her clear eyes, dark and deep with the intensity of her fervour, rested on Julian, as though they saw him and him only in all the world. Then her voice rang out again, sweet and full.

"There's no such thing as fate," she said. "Not like that! Not fate that makes us bad. There's God, Julian! It's trying to do right that matters; nothing else in life; and that we can all do. There's nothing, nothing can prevent us! Oh, I don't say"—her voice broke into a great pity and tenderness—"I don't say that it's not harder for some than for others. But it's what's hard that is best worth doing! Julian!"—she drew a step nearer to him, stretching out both her hands—"you're looking at it wrong, dear! The things you've lost for good are not the things that matter. What one has, what people think of one—that's nothing. It's what one is, it's oneself that's the only thing to mind about."

She stopped, her whole face stirred and tremulous with her conviction, and Julian, with an impulsive movement, caught her hands in his, and pressed his forehead down upon them in a blind agony of self-abasement.

"I'm a swindler, Clemmie!" he cried thickly. It was as though he had hardly taken in the full sense of her words, but was clinging to her, and confessing to her under some blunted, bewildered impetus. "A cheat and a thief all round! That's what I am!"

"But that's not for ever!" she cried, such love, and hope, and courage shining in her eyes as would not let her great tears fall. "You can retrieve the past! You can repent and begin again. Ah, I know, of course, that what is done can't ever be undone! What you have done remains the same for always! But you can change! You can be different, and nothing else but you yourself matters at all! What does it matter if people think you a cheat if you are an honest man? Nothing! No more than it matters to yourself if they call you an honest man for ever, when you're a cheat!" She paused again, but this time he did not speak; he lifted his head and drew her to him, crushing her hands against his breast, and looking into her eyes with a strange, agonised struggle towards comprehension dawning in his own.

There was a moment's dead silence. There was that passing between Clemence and Julian which no words could have touched—the final struggle towards dominion of a man's better nature. Falconer had fallen back. All that was narrow and conventional about his morality had shrivelled into nothingness, and stood confessed to his own consciousness for what it was.

He knew that the great question now at issue was beyond the reach of his man's practicality, and that he could only stand aside.

Mrs. Romayne was gripping heavily at the chair by which she stood; impotent, frozen despair paralysing her from head to foot, leaving alive and sentient only her eyes.

"You must go back, dear." The words fell from Clemence's lips tender, distinct, immutable as the laws of right and wrong. "You must take the consequences of what you've done, and through that pain and shame you'll get above it to begin again."

Julian's lips, white now as ashes, moved stiffly.

"The consequences?" he whispered. "The consequences, Clemmie?"

"The consequences," she replied, and in the ring of her voice, in the clasp with which her hands closed over his, was all the courage and conviction with which she sought to nerve him. "Ah, I don't know—I don't understand—but are there no innocent people who may suffer for your fault unless you are there to take it on yourself? Besides, how else, dear? How can you begin again without having made amends? How can you free yourself of the past without acknowledging what's black and bad in it? And if you acknowledge what's black and bad, how can you hesitate to take its punishment?"

And as if that struggling life in him were growing and stirring under her influence, a strange flickering light crept into Julian's face and the struggle in his eyes grew into a faint suggestion of victory. He paused a moment, his breath coming thick and fast.

"But suppose—suppose it isn't any good?" His voice, tense, hardly audible, seemed to catch and strain like that of a man at the very crisis of his life. "Suppose it's in me and I must——"

"It isn't so!" she cried, and as she spoke she drew away from him as though carried beyond herself, beyond her womanly love for him, in that supreme declaration of the truth that was her very being. "You know it isn't so! There is no 'must' except God's 'must' to us that we should follow Him. There is no power can tear us from His hand unless we throw ourselves away by saying that His hand is without strength to save us. Good and evil lie before every one of us, and we must all choose. And nothing else is real and living in this life except that choice and the end to which it leads us!"

Through all the limitations of the phraseology in which her faith was clothed, the great truth which makes the mystery of humanity, the truth which words can only belittle and obscure, which lives not in words but in the silent consciousness of each man's soul, rang out, all-penetrating and all-dominating. And as she faced him, her eyes shining, her whole face radiant, Julian caught her in his arms with a great cry.

"I will," he cried. "Clemence, I choose. Help me! I will go back."

She yielded to his touch, with a low sob, and as they stood clasped in one another's arms, a shuddering moan rang through the room, and Mrs. Romayne fell heavily forward at their feet.

CHAPTER XVI

"WILL she suffer any more?"

On the upper landing of the hotel in which Falconer had found Julian, Clemence was standing, one hand resting on the handle of a door which she had just closed behind her, looking in the uncertain light of a flickering gas-jet into the face of the man to whom she spoke. He was a quick, capable-looking man, with a brisk, professional manner, evidently a doctor. Clemence's face was pale and tired, as though with strain or watching, and her low voice shook a little. The doctor was drawing on his left-hand glove, and he paused to answer her.

"I should say that she would not," he said. "It is practically over." He gave a keen, rather curious look at Clemence and then added: "You are alone with the lady?"

"Yes," said Clemence simply.

A long night and a long day had passed, and between Mrs. Romayne and the one absorbing passion of her life had fallen that solemn shadow before which all earthly passions pale and fade away; that solemn shadow before whose creeping touch not strength of will, not love itself, can stand. As she fell to the ground before her son she had loosed her hold perforce on all the struggle and burning resolution which was life to her; she had followed the guide whom none may resist into that valley through which every one must pass, and its mists had lifted from her no more. From that one long faint she had been brought back only to fall into another; in such total unconsciousness, which had yielded twice to intervals of physical pain terrible to see, the long hours had passed.

And in one of these spaces of blank unconsciousness Julian Romayne had seen his mother for the last time. The necessity for his departure was pressing and relentless. The meeting of the shareholders was imminent, and that meeting he must face. He had left his mother's room in the grey light of the early morning with a look on his face which Clemence, the only witness of that mute parting, never forgot; and he had gone away with Dennis Falconer to make those preparations for his surrender of himself to justice which were not to be delayed.

And now the day was drawing to a close. The doctor had paid his last visit, and the night was drawing on.

There was a moment's pause after Clemence's words. Then the doctor wished her a professional good-night, and, as he went downstairs, she turned and went back into the room.

It was a small room, the best which the hotel cared to place at the disposal of sudden illness, but somewhat dingy and ill-appointed. The gaslight, shaded from the face upon the bed, but shedding a garish light upon the rest of the room, touched nothing luxurious, nothing which its present occupant could have realised in connection with herself. Her very rings lying upon the dressing-table and flashing under the gaslight, seemed to protest against such poor surroundings.

But the figure on the bed lay motionless, protesting never more. It lay in blank unconsciousness even when Clemence, crossing the room, stood for a moment looking down, her whole face tender and quivering, and then sank gently on her knees and pressed her lips, with a womanly gesture of infinite pity, to the pale, inanimate hand upon the bed. It was over now, practically, as the doctor, looking at that waning life from a purely physical point of view, had said—all the struggle and the dread, all the courage and the hope, the valiant ignorance of twenty years. And the face upon the pillow was the face of the vanquished—the face of one whose last vivid consciousness of earthly things had been the consciousness of failure.

For many minutes Clemence knelt there, all the feeling of her woman's soul seeming to expend itself in that soft, mute pressure. Then she rose quietly and moved across the room to make some final preparation for the night. That done, she came back again to the bedside, and doing so she started. The shadowy hands were moving feebly upon the counterpane. From out the grey, pinched face upon the pillow two glazed blue eyes were looking with a restless, searching movement as though in want of something. They rested upon Clemence with no recognition in them; but as her son's wife drew nearer to her quickly and gently, Mrs. Romayne moved feebly and tried to turn her head upon the pillow, as though moved by some vague, indefinite, and far-away sense of dislike and repulsion. Her white lips moved uncertainly as she did so, and faint sounds came from between them. Clemence bent over her tenderly and tried to catch the words; and they grew gradually a little clearer.

"My boy!" the faint, uncertain voice muttered, "my little boy!"

A great wave of pity and yearning swept over Clemence, and she sank once more to her knees, fixing her eyes on the poor, worn face. Was it of any use to speak? Could her voice reach to those dim lands where the mother groped for her "little boy"?

"He will come!" she said. "He will come—by-and-by!"

As though the voice had roused her without penetrating to her brain, Mrs. Romayne moved again—that slight, feeble movement so eloquent of the extremity of weakness. Her eyes turned to Clemence with that glance of vague, unrecognising dislike.

"No," she said, as though answering her—"no, he's too little." She paused, and again there was that groping movement of her hands. "His letter," she muttered, "his letter! My dear mamma! my dear mamma!"

There was a restless distress in the glazed eyes now, and their glance tore Clemence's heart. The feeble hands were moving painfully, and as she watched, with her tears falling fast in her impotent pity and longing to satisfy their craving, something in their movements, all unmeaning as they seemed at first, penetrated to Clemence's understanding with one of those strange flashes of comprehension only possible under so tense a strain of sympathy. Those nerveless hands were feeling for a pocket! In an instant Clemence had risen, crossed the room, and put her hand into the pocket of the dress which Mrs. Romayne had worn. Her finger touched a paper, and she drew it out instantly. She saw that it was yellow and faded with age, and she moved quickly back with it to the bedside. The hands and the eyes were still moving, but the muttered words were audible no longer, and as Clemence put the paper gently between the thin fingers, she felt with a sudden thrill of awe that they were growing cold.

But the touch seemed to rouse Mrs. Romayne once more. Her fingers closed on the paper as if instinctively, and the restless distress died out of her eyes as she tried—vainly—to unfold the paper. Clemence put out her hand gently, and did the work for which the dying fingers had no strength, and on the dying face there dawned a pale, shadowy smile.

"Yes!" she said. "Yes! 'My dear mamma!' My dear mamma! Your loving—son—Julian!"

And with her son's name on her lips, Mrs. Romayne left him behind, and passed from ignorance to knowledge.

The trial and conviction of Julian Romayne were a nine days' wonder in society. The people who had most readily and carelessly received the widow and son of William Romayne, asked one another with the martyred air of those whose charity has been abused and their feelings for morality outraged, what was to be expected after all of the son of such a father? The people whose feelings for morality had been outraged at the outset by Mrs. Romayne's reappearance in London, and soothed subsequently by the simplicity of the position, observed sagely that they had always said so. Both parties were unanimous in the assertion that the young man's life was practically at an end. He had forfeited his place in society for ever.

But Julian himself realised gradually and painfully during the years of his punishment; with the strength of a manhood attained through pain, when he went away to a new country with his wife and child; that his life had just begun.

THE END

Milton Keynes UK
Ingram Content Group UK Ltd.
UKHW030742071024
449371UK00006B/638